OBSESSIVE LOVE

*Other books by Liz Hodgkinson
published by Piatkus*

The Alexander Technique
Reincarnation
Spiritual Healing
Codependency (with David Stafford)

OBSESSIVE LOVE

*How to free
your emotions
and live again*

LIZ HODGKINSON

PIATKUS

© 1991 Liz Hodgkinson

First published in 1991 by
Judy Piatkus (Publishers) Ltd
5 Windmill Street, London W1P 1HF

**The moral right of the author
has been asserted**

*A catalogue record for this book is available
from the British Library*

ISBN 0 – 7499 – 1105 – 0

Edited by Esther Jagger
Designed by Sue Ryall

Set in Compugraphic Times by
Action Typesetting, Gloucester
Printed and bound in Great Britain by
Bookcraft Ltd, Midsomer Norton

To Veronica

Acknowledgments

This book was written with the help and kind support of many people. Apart from my therapist Veronica Stephenson, to whom this book is dedicated, for expert advice I should also like to thank psychotherapist Vera Diamond and anthropologist Branko Bokun.

Friends who gave helpful input are: Dr Penny Allan, Annie Halliday, my former husband Neville Hodgkinson and Ken Umpleby. Thanks are due, too, to the very many people who poured out their own stories of obsessive love, helping to shed light on this peculiar and distressing phenomenon.

I should also like to record my gratitude to John, the 'victim' of my own obsessive love, for his tolerance and wisdom, and his understanding of a difficult situation.

Contents

A Hopeless, Helpless Passion

This book is for you if you are, or have ever been, caught in the grip of an overwhelming but hopeless, helpless passion. It is for all those who have loved desperately and besottedly, but have not had their love returned; those for whom loving has ever caused far more agony and anguish than ecstasy. It is for those who once had a wild crush or infatuation for somebody and who, years later, still cannot seem to get thoughts of this person out of their minds. It is for those who may feel resentment, bitterness and hostility for many years, even decades, after a one-sided affair finished.

It is also for the 'victims' − those who have been on the unwilling receiving end of somebody else's besottedness, and have felt powerless to understand or deal with it, or who have perhaps become frightened by the sheer intensity of the other person's emotions. I hope it will be useful as well for people who would like to try and understand that mysterious, all-compelling, all-consuming and often self-destructive force that we know as obsessive love.

For almost the whole of written history obsessive love has been regarded as a grand passion, as high drama, as the raw material of so much literature. So many of us have agonized when the world's great fictional and factual lovers have seen their hopes and longings turn to dust and ashes because the loved one does not respond, or when declarations of passion have been met with a wall of indifference. We have wept with them as their love has been frustrated, and their attentions continually spurned and reviled or misunderstood by the beloved. Shakespeare's Othello fell victim to obsessive love. The object of his obsession, Desdemona, simply could not understand how he felt – and was murdered for her lack of comprehension. In later works of literature, Flaubert's Emma Bovary and Tolstoy's Anna Karenina loved hopelessly and tragically. In real life, Charlotte Brontë nursed an anguished, unrequited passion for her Belgian teacher, Professor Heger – an agonizing experience that she poured into two of her novels, *The Professor* and *Villette*.

Many successful films have had obsessive love as their theme. The 1971 film *Play Misty for Me*, starring the young Clint Eastwood, has as its theme the uncontrollable infatuation of a young girl for a radio DJ. The mid-eighties' box office sensation *Fatal Attraction* turned this same theme into almost unwatchable horror. And, of course, one of the greatest movie successes of all time, *Gone with the Wind*, though having the American Civil War as its backdrop, is given its drama by the theme of obsessive love. Throughout the film and the runaway bestselling book we see how Scarlett O'Hara's machinations, her energy, are fuelled by her unrequited passion for Ashley Wilkes. Everything she does is for him; yet he remains bemused and mystified – and passionless.

From time to time we read stories in the newspapers of people who have become besotted, who commit mad or dangerous acts while in the grip of their wild obsession for another person. Ruth Ellis, the last woman to be hanged in Britain, died because of her obsessive, unrequited love for David Blakely. On reading these stories we may imagine that we, living much more sedate and ordinary lives, have never been through anything so searing, so agonizing, as this. But the chances are that many, if not most, of us will have had at least one experience of such 'high drama' in our lives – an unhappy, unsatisfactory experience of love which has left us confused and bewildered, and which never seems quite to vanish.

You are, or have been, prey to obsessive love if:

- Your feelings alternate wildly between love and hate
- You have ever felt you might faint in the presence of the loved one
- Your friends, family and work seem to fade into insignificance beside the loved one

- You find yourself haunting, stalking, writing to or phoning the loved one incessantly
- The object of your affections seems to respond with indifference, or seems to hate or try to avoid you
- You feel tongue-tied and awkward in the loved one's presence
- You would like to have this person all to yourself, perhaps even to the extent of locking him or her up
- You have a feeling of isolation, that nobody understands, that nobody has ever suffered like you
- You feel you are gradually losing your identity
- Your health has suffered
- Thoughts of the loved one dominate your every moment
- You feel that the loved one is not on the plane of normal, ordinary human beings but something set apart
- You feel that the loved one has the power to confer on you both lasting, unalloyed happiness and terrible misery
- You have fallen madly in love with somebody you don't even know, somebody who is completely unattainable, or somebody to whom you have never even spoken.

Even something so apparently simple, harmless and universal as a crush on a prefect or teacher at school, or a yearning to see and be with a pop star, may constitute a mild form of obsessive love.

If your own particular experience of 'high drama' happened a long time ago, you may be tempted to imagine that it is all now safely in the past, all but forgotten. You may even believe that an early or hopeless infatuation was just a stepping-stone on the way to a more mature and equal love – a try-out or, perhaps, an episode you now feel ashamed of and would rather not recall.

If you are currently caught up in the vortex you may believe, tell yourself, or be told that one day you will get over it and laugh about it, that it's something which happens to everybody and is nothing to worry about. Your friends or your mother may tell you that one day you will find the right man or woman, who loves you back, one who is worthy of you. But you don't believe them.

When obsessive love happens to us, we tend to minimize

and deny it. We are ashamed of ourselves. We hate ourselves for going so far out of control. We cannot understand what is happening, and as often as not we try to pretend that it is not happening. We may even declare to others that we don't love this person, that he or she means nothing to us. The temptation is to stuff the feelings down, to try and block them out, to carry on with normal life and wait for it all to be over so that calmness can once more descend.

The psychological effects

But now, it is increasingly being understood by psychologists that, whenever such very strong emotions overwhelm us, they may well constitute a serious psychological trauma which can threaten to blight and cast a baleful influence over the rest of our lives. It is also being realized that until the trauma is addressed, faced and brought out into the open it will never go away. It doesn't matter how long ago an incident of obsessive love happened, or how far down into the subconscious it has been pushed, if it once knocked you sideways the effects may last a very long time.

Experiencing an incident of obsessive love is a bit like having a driving accident in which you dent your car. The car is still drivable, and in time you may forget about the dent and get used to the car's appearance. But until you take it into a garage to have it repaired that dent will always be there. Falling victim to obsessive love constitutes a 'dent' in the psyche which will remain there for as long as you try to forget about it and pretend it never happened.

The experience may well cast a dark shadow across all later relationships too. They will be coloured and affected by the incident. It is more than likely that an incident of obsessive love will have the effect of blocking off and freezing future feelings, so that ever afterwards responses to other people are blunted. There may well be difficulties with relating and empathizing, or even in having successful intimate relationships.

It's as if, having fallen prey to these feelings once, we make up our minds that we will never be so hurt and humiliated again. For a time this attitude may act as a survival mechanism, but it can also make us seem hard and cold to others. And inside ourselves we may know that there's always something holding us back from full commitment, full love, full empathy. We no longer know how to *feel*. And that is the great tragedy of falling victim to this kind of passion – it blocks off the ability to feel properly.

Trying to forget about those who have obsessed us simply doesn't work. In fact, it seems that the more we try to erase them from the memory, the more likely it is that thoughts of them will return and haunt us in our thoughts and dreams. That is why so many people carry to the grave a secret longing for the person who first aroused their passions – and often die with that person's name on their lips even if the affair happened fifty years earlier. Or a traumatic incident in later life may recall vivid thoughts of this one, special lover.

Not long ago I, like many people, imagined that besotted, unrequited love was something which happened only to exceptionally intense and perhaps unstable people, those whose lives were lived on a more vivid and uncomfortable plane than average. It did not, I was sure, happen to level-headed, stable and non-neurotic individuals. I thought at one time that people who fell prey to obsessive love were at least slightly unhinged. Now I believe that this kind of 'love' can itself unhinge us, and actually make us mentally and emotionally unstable and behave in ways which may seem completely uncharacteristic – at least for a time.

I believe that anybody can fall obsessively in love, and that nobody can guarantee to be immune. It also seems reasonably certain that, for most people, such an incident of obsession happens only once in a lifetime. It does not tend to be a repeating pattern, something which happens over and over again – thank goodness! For anybody who has ever been through it, once is absolutely enough. Although it is often associated with growing up and adolescence, obsessive love is by no means confined to the young. It can strike at any age. And more often than not it comes as a bolt out of the blue – it strikes us as with a lightning flash. Having recently accessed, relived and admitted my own painful, obsessive, unrequited love affair, the impact of which cast a baleful influence over my life for more than a quarter of a century, I am left wondering whether there is anybody who *hasn't* at some time experienced such a passion – even if only apparently for a short time.

Secret lives

Until I started speaking to friends and acquaintances about my own affair, I seemed to have met nobody in 'real life' who had suffered from obsessive love. Now I know that this kind of love is something that people rarely mention in ordinary conversation. Like Shakespeare's lady who sat smiling at grief, they never tell their love but let concealment feed on their damask cheeks. But once I gave people 'permission' to talk by mentioning my own affair, I found the stories came pouring out.

So many apparently settled and happily married men and women, pillars of society, living respectable, affluent, successful lives, have told me that there is somebody whom they just cannot forget, somebody for whom they still secretly yearn. Occasionally there has been an affair, a relationship of sorts, some element of coming together, with this other person. Sometimes the obsession has happened only at long distance, and the sufferer has never even spoken to the object of the obsession. In some cases there has been a marriage or other long-term relationship. But in all cases, without exception, the relationship has ended in disaster. Love turns to hate, obsession may turn to depression, hostility or long-term resentment. But however unsatisfactory the relationship has been, other, later relationships seem pale and insignificant by contrast.

One woman I met wore two wedding rings, one on her 'ring finger' and the other on her right hand. She said: 'That ring never, ever leaves my finger. I would have my finger cut off rather than remove that ring.' It was given to her by her first husband, a handsome rake whom she married at the age of seventeen and who left her with a small child not long afterwards. She has not even seen him for nearly thirty years – but says that not a day goes by when she doesn't think of him, yearn for him, long for him. Her present husband, a steady, nice, stable, loving man, has never been able to excite her passions in the same way – although she acknowledges that he makes a far better husband. But although she has tried and tried, she cannot stop thoughts of this early, unsatisfactory love from returning to haunt her.

I met a professional colleague at a party with her recent husband. They seemed happy enough, and well suited. They are both lecturers at the same college, in the same subject. But as we got talking Mandy confessed that she could not get a previous lover out of her mind. He was somebody I had met. 'Didn't you find him amazingly attractive?' she asked me eagerly. Following the usual pattern of obsessive love, she was besotted while he remained indifferent. (It's also a pattern that those who have been obsessed want everybody else to find the lover wonderful and extraordinary, as well.)

As it happens, although I hadn't found him attractive personally I could see that there was 'something' about him. There usually is − that's the trouble. It's often the case that those who have obsessed us are more striking, more handsome, more charismatic than ordinary − although not always.

Mark is middle-aged, highly successful in his work as a management consultant, and apparently happily married. Yet he confessed that for the past three years he has been obsessed by a neighbour, a woman he hardly knows. He drives past her house hoping for a glimpse of her, and follows her discreetly to the supermarket and to other parts of the town. He feels that one day he will have to declare his love − even though he will risk his marriage and possibly his job, not to mention the very great possibility of rejection.

Obsessive love is so searing, so cataclysmic, so uncontrollable. But what is it, exactly? How does it arise in the first place − and why do so very many of us fall victim? These are questions which this book seeks to answer. It also describes how − and why − the wound left by obsessive love *can* be healed, in fact, *must* be healed if we are to live the rest of our lives freed from its chains.

Along with therapists and counsellors working in this field, I believe that obsessive love, rather than being just a more intense and uncomfortable version of falling in love, is actually pathological, unhealthy, and something which needs to be sorted out if we are to live the rest of our lives fully. I do not believe it bears any relation to real love at all, and that in many ways it is the complete opposite. It seems to me that we have been rather misled by poetry and drama into believing that obsessive love is a grand passion, and something which is, in its way, even ennobling. Poets and dramatists have often chosen obsessive love as their theme, probably because it is the most dramatic thing that can ever happen to a human being. Nothing else can take you over, possess and overwhelm you to quite the same extent. Nothing else can so skew normal life. Nothing else can make you behave in such shameful ways. Nothing else can make you go so out of control.

But though great writers have accurately described the pain, they have had difficulty in understanding it. And certainly they have never given any advice to sufferers on how to deal with it. Psychologists too have had difficulty in coming to terms with it, and there is very little psychological literature or research on the subject.

Obsessive love seems to stand alone. It refuses to be categorized and pinned down in the same way as 'women who love too much', for example. From study after study it has emerged that women who 'love too much' tend to form dysfunctional relationships with addicted or abusive men and to come from certain types of unhealthy family backgrounds. Such women (and men too) become addicted to people whom they feel they can rescue and save from themselves. But there seems no such parallel motivation or pattern in obsessive love. It strikes right out of the blue, and then overtakes the mind and spirit completely, putting all normal behaviour into abeyance. Its very mystery is one of the reasons why it has excited, and continues to excite, so many novelists, dramatists and poets. So is it just one of those things, something we can never really hope to understand?

I thought so once. But now I believe that new insights, new work on the impact of trauma, can give us for the first time detailed understanding of this peculiar phenomenon. Also, new therapies can help us to heal the wound, and to live the rest of our lives without that dark, painful shadow in the background. I believe that with obsessive love, time is no healer at all. The experience of obsessive love can be likened to dropping a stitch in knitting, and never picking it up. The knitting never looks quite right from then on, unless we unpick it and start again from the mistake. Luckily, these days, it is possible to unravel the knitting of the rest of our lives, correct the mistake and shed the burden.

Through telling my own story and those of other people who have been in sometimes frightening thrall to such a passion, and through listening to the stories of those who have been on the receiving end — which can be just as traumatic — I hope that this book will shed some clear light on the subject, and give useful strategies for releasing the trauma from the system. We cannot always choose not to fall obsessively in love — in fact, we probably never do choose it. We don't choose to be hurt or humiliated, or to love those who don't love us back. We don't choose to have our feelings spurned and reviled. But we *can* recover from its stranglehold, free ourselves and learn how to replace obsessions with genuine, lasting feelings of love.

Part One

DEFINING THE PROBLEM

1 Secrets from the Past

The glamour of notoriety

I shall begin with an account of my own experience of obsessive love, partly because I know it so well, but also because it provides a copybook example of how the whole process seems to operate. It also shows why it can fester in the system long after the affair is apparently forgotten.

I met John in my first term at university. I had gone straight from school and an extremely sheltered existence in East Anglia. Like most girls in the early sixties, I longed to fall headily in love and to find a man who would be worthy of that great prize – relieving me of my virginity. Even so, I was unprepared for the impact that meeting John would have. When I first saw him, he was standing near the front of a queue in the canteen. I was immediately attracted: not only was he tall, dark and extremely handsome in a poetic, saturnine style, but he seemed much older than the other students. He looked experienced, confident – and infinitely intriguing.

'Who is he?' I asked Bob, the boy I was with – somebody who had been plaguing me for weeks but whom I longed to shake off.

'Don't you know?' he asked, surprised. 'That's John.' Bob went on to inform me that John, although in his first term like me, was already famous – or notorious. He had defied the then strict dress rules for his first formal dinner in Hall, and had gone in wearing a huge floppy pink silk bow tie. He also had a reputation for being something of a rake. He was older than most first-year students, Bob added, telling me that John had worked as a teacher in a prep school abroad (which seemed extremely glamorous) and had been a medical student.

The more Bob told me, the more fascinated I became. I looked a little more closely at this striking young man. He had a wing of jet-black hair, clean-cut features and also a slightly decadent, world-weary air. His dress set him apart from the other male students, who in those days mostly wore tweed jackets, grey flannels and Bri-nylon shirts. John was wearing a huge black handknitted sweater coming almost to his knees and a stripey scarf – not a university one, naturally.

It may be an exaggeration to say that I fell hopelesly in love with John simply on seeing him in this queue, but from then on his image began to obsess me. I couldn't get him out of my head. To me, he seemed the most glamorous young man I had ever encountered and somehow I had to have him. But how? How could I ever get to meet him, to let him know I was interested?

There was only one thing to do: stalk him, find out the places where he was likely to be, and make sure I was there as well. I forgot my work entirely and concentrated on trying to get a glimpse of that vision once more. But for weeks, as it seemed, my efforts went unrewarded. I just never saw him around at all. Of course, it was impossible to ask anybody where he might be – they might suspect I was unduly interested. I never told a soul, and wondered when or whether I would ever see him again. All the time, the obsession grew stronger – and this was somebody I had so far never even spoken to, somebody who did not even know I existed.

Then one day, when I was working in the library, my efforts were rewarded. There He was, standing by the window looking something up in a book. I can still remember the impact he had on me – he seemed to be clothed in light, a young god temporarily descended from Mount Olympus to inhabit this prosaic university. How had He come to be here? Somehow I had to go and speak to him, make myself known to him. Nothing remotely like this had ever happened to me before. I did not know how to behave, but seemed propelled by something outside myself. Already I felt as if I was possessed, that some alien had invaded my body, making me act in all kinds of uncharacteristic ways. I could not control what I did.

As I sat and watched him sit down at his place in the library, my stomach churned. He glanced over at me and I smiled at him, signalling that I was interested. He smiled back. My God! At that, my whole being was inflamed and I started making eyes at him. Before long, I got up from my table and went over to speak to him.

I introduced myself and found him to be pleasant, if rather distant, and quite talkative. We opened up a conversation of sorts – already I was transported – and eventually, for some reason, he saw me to the bus stop. By this time I was in an altered state of consciousness and didn't feel at all at ease or comfortable with myself. I had made contact – but now what?

Overtures spurned

I so much wanted to impress him, and yet I had the feeling he wasn't impressed at all, just coolly polite. When I got home, misery and desolation descended. Also, a feeling of fear knotted the pit of my stomach. But this was also mixed with a kind of wild elation, as I recorded in my diary on 12 November 1962: 'Made progress with John – tall, dashing, marvellous, handsome. We sat in the Arts Reading Room nearly all the morning, at intervals staring at each other and smiling.' But the following day I wrote:

I looked in vain all over college today for John and consequently had a miserable, frustrating time since I didn't see him and to make it worse saw Bob not once but three times, stonily staring at me. [I had ditched Bob, of course, to make way for John.] I wasn't really there at the lecture: thoughts fixed on John, John, all the time. Oh John, John, I must get him out of my mind. Why have I fallen for him like this? We are both [my flatmate and myself] in bed now early and

5

Penny is falling asleep and I am wide awake thinking about John all the time. And I have hardly spoken to him. Oh John, why, why, why?

Some sixth sense already told me that he was not interested, that he never would be, and that my feelings would not be returned. But the obsession grew stronger and I was not in the slightest bit put off by his indifference.

By 19 November, with things very little advanced, I was getting desperate. I wrote:

John, John, John. I think endlessly about him and have done for days. I love him, truly love him as I have never loved another man. Pure pleasure at the mere sight of him and yet why, why, why do I love him when I know he doesn't love me and probably never will, not lasting love anyway, as I have for him.

One way of getting to know him a bit better of course, was to invite him to a party – then as now, an 'okay' way for a girl to ask a young man to a social function. As I hadn't got any parties to invite him to, the thing was to hold one of my own with my flatmate. The party was going to be my golden opportunity to let John know for certain how I felt. I invited him, and recorded in my diary: 'Marvellously, he accepted.' Penny and I got in a barrel of beer and some simple food and waited for the guests to arrive. Most of them turned up fairly on time – except, of course, for John. My agony was unbearable, beyond enduring. He isn't going to come, I told myself. He isn't going to come.

But eventually he did. He wore, as I recorded, one blue sweater, one black sweater, and an orange and grey stripey handknitted tie which made his shirt collar stand up Edwardian-fashion. Despair turned instantly to bliss as I opened the door to him: I forgot all about my other guests and concentrated entirely on John. He was the only one I wanted to be with – all the others were makeweights.

I showed John into the living room, he had some beer – and then we went upstairs to the bedroom. We stayed together there for hours and hours. I wrote in my diary:

I knew then that I had never found any man so absolutely physically attractive, with complete lack of inhibitions and charming suavity. And absolute bliss on the bed with him . . . he is the first man for a long time I have desired so absolutely physically as a man . . . such absolute perfect happiness for the few hours he was here, smoking my tipped cigarettes and drinking our beer. The wonderful thrill of HIM.

I was almost ready for sex with him, but it did not quite happen on this occasion – mainly through fears of other people walking into the bedroom. But if anything set the final seal on my obsession, this evening was it.

The trouble was, John made no effort to see me again. He seemed to have enjoyed the party, he appeared to have found me quite attractive, but did not ask me out or seek my company. My diary entries after the party record increasing desperation and despair. On 25 November, I wrote: 'Longing and longing and longing for John.' And on the following day: 'The longing to see John is as great as ever, to see that young, ravaged face.'

By this time my whole being was taken up with trying to see John; not necessarily even to speak to him, just to see him. In the event, another week or two of 'longing' went by before I saw him again, in the library as before. I took another plunge and invited him to another party. He accepted, and although he still never asked me out, or hinted that he'd like a proper relationship, he was intensifying his efforts to get me to go to bed with him. 'You only go so bloody far,' he had said on one occasion.

Although I had made up my mind that John met all the criteria of 'worthiness' that my first lover had to fulfil, the prospect of going to bed with him complicated the whole issue. I knew I could not refuse for ever, but wished he would show a little more interest in me as a person. I now think that John was trying to put me off, to let me know that he wasn't interested. But, like so many young men, he would not pass up the chance of sex, if it was on offer. He was probably as bewildered and confused by my behaviour as I was, but had no strategies for coping with it. He may have been somewhat flattered, even intrigued, but could not return my strong feelings.

Ignoring everything else in life

Life for me became a kind of hell. My academic work didn't just suffer – it vanished. I spent no time on cultivating other friendships, and had no female friends except my flatmate Penny. My lecturers and others who knew me thought I was promiscuous, sex-mad, a man-chaser. Because I dressed flamboyantly in those days and appeared bold (only to attract John), other young men flocked round me – I ignored them. I must have created an awful impression, because one of my lecturers remarked to somebody that he must be the only man in the university who hadn't been to bed with me. So far from the truth – yet it was a reputation that was to take me a year or more to shake off.

Whenever I was in John's presence I gazed at him with a kind of soppy adoration, which must have got on his nerves. However he never said anything, and I never told him how very much I loved him (for it did truly feel like love); neither of us ever talked anything through, which would have been the sensible thing to do. He probably just hoped I'd get fed up and go away, but his indifference and coldness had the exact opposite effect – it made me even more determined to be with him and yes, to sleep with him.

The obsession grew unabated. On 1 December I wrote in my diary (my only real friend at the time):

I still think about him all the time and know damn well that he doesn't care a fig about me. He's absolutely ruthless and unscrupulous [I had been told this by one of his 'friends' and wanted to believe it] and I know it and I still long to see him but don't want to. Strange mixed-up feelings about him.

On 6 December, now getting near the end of term, I saw him again at a party:

At about half past eleven he turned up and I felt absolutely blissfully, ecstatically happy. Don't dote, I was told, but I do, even though he hates me now, through desire unfulfilled. Even so, he is still marvellous. With him, a never-before feeling. Oh I do love you John. I must do. Why else have

I been thinking of nothing else for over a month now? Everyone seems to be aware of the attraction except him, and he thinks I'm playing with him. The absolute, absolute attraction he has for me ... I have never loved anyone like him before. If only, if only I could go away with him for Christmas and then, then, just he and I could be with each other. When he is around I see and note no one else. I must get over this longing and desire for him which may ultimately endanger my university career.

It seems from this entry as if I did have some inkling that this was a dangerous obsession, but I was powerless to take note of the warning signs. I had asked John to so many parties and functions, yet still he never asked me to anything. It became so completely one-sided that in the end I grew nervous of asking him to anything else.

In the meantime, intrigued by the strength of my feelings towards John, several other young men who were friends of his were showing interest and asking me out, in some cases to enable me to 'get over him'. Vain hope! But in any case I wasn't attracted to any of them, and going out with them only served to heighten my longing for John, as they reminded me of him.

By this time I had invested John, whom I still hardly knew, with a demonic persona. He became Lucifer, the brightest of the angels, now descended into darkness; he was the embodiment of dark desires, the unacceptable, frightening personification of sex, elemental man. The probability that he was just a very young, insecure man simply not able to handle the situation never occurred to me. I believed − wanted to believe − that he was playing cat and mouse with me for his own dastardly purposes. I never had the mental or emotional freedom to ask myself what effect my constant stalking and haunting might be having on him. My lack of empathy with him and his situation was total.

In fact, when caught in the grip of an overwhelming obsession there never is any empathy with the other person, as I later discovered. One major characteristic of obsessive love is that it is completely selfish. The other is that its victims are incapable of rational thought and behaviour. On 10 December I recorded feeling 'white hot' desire for John, and hoped that he might invite me to an end of term dance at his hall of residence. I knew it was unlikely, and he didn't. Instead he invited someone else, as one of his friends kindly informed me. Bitter rage, more despair, more agony as I imagined him with this other girl. I bravely wrote: 'I don't care how many girls he has so long as I'm one of them.'

Then one of my lecturers, a young man recently down from Cambridge, invited me to a party at his house. John was not asked, but one of his friends assured me that he would crash the party later and get John to come as well. I felt ecstatic again and wrote: 'It will be a marvellous party with getting drunk and John and consummation, which I am determined about even if he has got another girl. I could have loads of men myself were it not for the mad passion.' Unfortunately it was not a marvellous party − not for me at any rate. By the time John arrived − horrifically late as usual − I was so drunk that all I could do was fall in a heap at his feet. The evening was a terrible nightmare, ending in tears, despair and aloneness.

I now tried very hard to forget him, to put the whole unsatisfactory episode behind me. On 15 December I wrote in my diary: 'Thank God I'm going off him, I think.' No chance. That Christmas, with nothing achieved, I thought only of John all the time, and could hardly wait to get back to university for the start of the new term. When I mentioned the incident recently to my mother, she said, 'Oh yes, I remember John.' I told her she had never met him and knew nothing about him. Then she reminded me that during that Christmas vacation I had been able to talk of nothing else. 'You were absolutely full of him,' she said.

In my diary, I gave myself some extremely sensible advice: 'I promise myself that next term will be different. I shall meet different people and try to forget the memory and image (still vivid, unfortunately) of the glamorous and rotten John, the association with whom is entirely my own fault and I have no one else to blame at all.' It was no use. I could not forget him. At the beginning of the next term I hung around and stalked him as intensely as ever − and at last he responded, not with affection, not with love, but with a typical young man's ultimatum: if I were serious about being so keen on him, then I would have to go to bed with him.

Imagined ecstasy

Of course, I had never for one minute let go of the belief that he was the 'worthy one' to initiate me into physical sex. And so it happened (at last!). One afternoon I went with a mixture of longing and dread to his hall of residence, where I would be relieved of my virginity. I was absolutely seized up with terror. Would it hurt? Would there be a lot of blood? I was also terrified of seeming inexperienced, and frightened because I knew John didn't love me and had no feelings of affection for me. His ultimatum came from a young man's urgent need for sex, and possibly from a lack of understanding that when a young and inexperienced girl seems seductive, this is simply because she does not know how else to show she is interested.

It took place on 20 January, 1963. I know this because the day afterwards I wrote an account of the experience. Reading it with hindsight, I realize it was far more what I wanted to believe happened than what actually took place:

Last night, culmination of love in − Hall, painful, searing, in heights of ecstasy with HIM − wonderfully, completely masculine. Inadequacy of words to express the exhilaration and fulfilment of last night ... utterly exhausting, trying to express physically what one feels. I long once again to have J. possess me but this time it will be more complete than before, having received initiation into the dark urges of the body and coming out on the other side. J. was cold-blooded, ruthless-seeming, amoral, but when alone how different, how utterly different. No more nights of loneliness, of desire ungratified. I love him.

In fact the experience was one of the most traumatic of my life, and if it was supposed to have brought us together it didn't succeed − it had the opposite effect. Far from fusing us in any way, the upshot of the afternoon and evening (the seduction

11

took several difficult hours to achieve) was that John never wanted to see me again.

I had thought that John was an experienced lover. But many years after this event he conceded that it had been painful and traumatic for him and said that the failure was due to his 'ineptness'. If only we could have talked it through then, my obsession with him might have worked itself out and disappeared. As it was, it became like an endless tape which couldn't be switched off, but ran round and round until years later I eventually managed to switch it off with the help of some skilful therapy.

So John cut me off completely, and I was shattered. He soon acquired a girlfriend, a proper one this time, and seemed to be very much in love with her. He didn't want to speak to me and I couldn't trust myself to speak to him. We were not to speak again, in fact, until December 1990 – when I met him at Heathrow Airport, Terminal Four, and we got on extremely well! But by that time I had at last conquered the obsession which had, without my really knowing it, affected the whole of my adult life.

I now had to try and pick up the pieces – but how? I was reading law, a subject I already hated, and had failed all my end of term exams. I froze towards John. Sometimes I saw him in the library, in the union, having a drink in the bar. But I never made any attempt to get near him. I had the overwhelming feeling that he had treated me shamefully, brutally, that he had treated me without compassion or sympathy. I for my part felt overcome with hurt and shame that I had become so obsessed and let my behaviour get so out of control. The phrase 'something in me died' has become a well-worn cliché, but that was how I felt. My very first attempts at love had been completely spurned.

Also, this man had taken my virginity – in those days it meant so much more than it does today, partly because we were terrified of pregnancy, and partly because it was so fiercely drummed into us that decent young men did not take advantage of girls before marriage. These attitudes were so completely overturned by the advent of the pill only a year or so later that it's hard to imagine they were current until so recently.

The subsequent trauma

I did not become pregnant, but my body went into a state of shock. The first sign of malaise was a distressing vaginal infection. It was probably thrush, but in my ignorance and terror I thought that John had given my syphilis and I hated him now even more. The infection made me feel dirty and used, and would not go away. I was too terrified to see a doctor about it, and it was months and months before it cleared up − of its own accord, probably when the severe stress and shock had receded somewhat. Nor was that my only health problem. My gums started bleeding − a common problem among young people when they are run down. I also had a mild attack of glandular fever.

Poor health, debilitating diseases and feelings of guilt and shame were bad enough, but they were not the only difficulties I had to face throughout that academic year. Because of the undesirable reputation I had acquired nobody wanted to go out with me now. And when Neville, who later became my husband, mentioned to a fellow student that he was attracted to me he was warned off. I was also eating badly, and drinking and smoking a lot; my finances were chaotic and I amassed a huge overdraft that I had no hope of paying off. My academic work was a disaster. I thought about applying to change from law to English, but this was complicated by the fact that John was reading English. What to do?

A sensible relationship

Then, later that term, Neville came into my life. I now think he saved me and helped me back from the brink. When I met him he was just nineteen, fresh-faced, tall, very slim and nice-looking with lots of blond curly hair. He could not have been more different from the saturnine, confident-seeming John, and I don't think quite honestly that Neville would have stood much of a chance if I hadn't been still reeling from the trauma of my relationship, if one can call it that, with John.

13

But Neville was, he declared, madly in love with me –
although we had never spoken before – and we got on bril-
liantly from the start. My life seemed to pick up. Gradually
my health improved and I was accepted to read English on
condition that I passed the end-of-year law exams (which I
surprised everybody by doing). John seemed to fade out of
the picture as my relationship with Neville became stronger
and culminated in our marriage while we were still students.

We later had two sons and entered the same profession –
daily newspaper journalism. We had a successful, compan-
ionable, equal marriage, though the incident with John lay
between us all throughout our marriage as something dark,
secret and highly traumatic which must be carefully skated
round, never disturbed, never spoken about, never brought
out into the open. For years I could not even mention John's
name. It was a name that was not allowed to be mentioned
by anybody. He was referred to, if at all, by both of us as
'that chap', and by Neville as, 'that man in your past'.

When we first met, Neville knew I was trying to recover
from a painful love affair and he saw John as some kind of
demon lover who had treated me brutally and shamefully. He
was not to change that impression for more than a quarter of
a century, although he hardly knew John at all.

Skeletons from the past

It might be imagined that, given Neville's love, given the secu-
rity and equality of our relationship, the incident with John
would gradually fade into insignificance. After all, I had never
had a proper relationship with him, had never even had what
one might call a genuine conversation. We had never exchanged
anything of meaning together. But the conclusion to this story
illustrates how very unlikely obsessions and traumas are to
disappear of their own accord – particularly if there was, as in
my case, a complete inability even to talk about it. Consciously,
of course, I hardly thought about John during those years. But
every now and again, for no apparent reason, a memory of
him would surface, accompanied by stomach-churning and
feelings of hatred, hostility and resentment. More than once

I had thought to myself: if ever I see that bugger again, I'll let him know how much he hurt and wounded me all those years ago. One day, I thought, I'll get even with him.

I knew that he had married, had a daughter and become a university lecturer. He had stayed for some years in the same town where we had both been at university, as had Neville and I, but we never had any communication. I do remember Neville saying once, on meeting John after we were all married with children, that he didn't seem so bad as I had painted him – that he appeared to be quite nice really. My own reaction was to snort in disbelief, and Neville left it there. From time to time I fantasized about how I would act if ever I did meet John again, which seemed extremely unlikely. So it never quite vanished. Then, in the summer of 1990, an incident, trivial in itself, had consequences which disturbed me and brought home the shattering truth that I was still suffering from the after-effects of the obsession.

By this time Neville and I had divorced, although remaining very good friends, and we were both living alone in flats in central London. Neither of us had remarried or formed any other relationship – nor did we want to. We were both happy to be single people again, leading our own independent lives.

For ten years before it finally ended our marriage had been celibate, by mutual consent. It may be imagined by some that my traumatic experience with John affected my ability to enjoy sex, and was, with hindsight, a reason for the celibacy. To me, this does not seem to be the case.

After the incident with John I had a number of affairs with different young men, experiencing varying levels of ecstasy, enjoyment, boredom and all the other emotions associated with a sexual relationship. It seems to me, from what I can gather from talking to people, that my own experiences of sex were pretty standard for our times – and that I am as capable as anybody else of enjoying sex, or of going off it. The reasons for choosing celibacy have, I believe, more to do with a perceived need for self-empowerment and solitude than with whether I have a 'low sex drive' or was traumatized by an early experience.

There were no further traumatic events, but what I can say after more than a decade of celibacy is that I have experienced a life without sex as one of liberation, of taking delight in my own autonomy and lack of dependence on anybody else. I also now believe that it was the years of voluntary celibacy which helped me finally to face the trauma of the past and to relive and release it. I doubt that it could have happened so easily if I had been in an intimate, sexual relationship with anybody.

My freedom from sex actually gave me the clarity needed to face up to these issues, and to be ready to deal with them when they arose and demanded some kind of solution. It would not have been easy, or perhaps even possible, with a possessive lover in the background. It is very likely, however, that the incident adversely affected my emotional responses towards people, which was why I was disturbed by what happened in August 1990.

I was standing in a queue to sign up for a yoga class near my home when I heard a strangely familiar voice behind me. I looked round and recognized an old boyfriend, somebody I had gone out with briefly when Neville and I had temporarily split up for a few months at university. Last time I had seen this chap he had been a fine-art student. Now he was a middle-aged, grey-haired man, dressed in a business suit and carrying a briefcase. He had become a chartered accountant.

After the yoga class I asked him round for a drink, and we caught up with each other's adult lives. Then he asked if he could have a walk round the garden, as it was a lovely summer's evening. As we walked round the large communal garden, my stomach started to churn uncomfortably and distressingly. I wondered: am I sexually attracted to him, or what? These strong feelings did not appear to be appropriate: we had only ever had a fairly casual relationship without any overwhelming attraction on either side or regrets when it all petered out.

Discovering therapy

As it happened, a couple of weeks later I visited a therapy centre in Scotland called Morning Light, which specializes in helping victims of child abuse and other serious traumas by encouraging them to access, relive and release painful incidents in the past. I had gone there for a story I was writing for a newspaper. But while I was there one of the therapists, Veronica Stephenson, asked me if I wanted any therapy myself. Of course, at the time I had no idea I had ever suffered from obsessive love, and so I said rather dismissively: 'If you like, but I don't think I've got any problems.' I mentioned, though, the recent incident with the former boyfriend I had met at yoga. 'Would the meeting with him make my stomach churn?' I asked Veronica.

She thought it was unlikely, especially if I had been pleased to see him, which I was, and if nothing traumatic or disturbing had happened between us in the past. It was more likely, she thought, that meeting him had triggered off a disturbing memory quite unrelated to him. She then started asking questions about what else had happened during that phase of my life. 'Well,' I said, somewhat hesitantly, 'I did have an unrequited love affair at about this time. Perhaps it could be that.' As we talked it became clear that the incident with John, short-lasting and unimportant as it seemed, had actually constituted a major trauma which had never gone away.

Recent work on the psychology of those who have suffered in air crashes, football disasters and so on has revealed that, unless the trauma is released, it stays in the system for years on end and affects everything in future life to some extent. Psychologists have found that, however long ago the trauma happened, it will never go away of its own accord. Whenever it has gone really deep, it needs expert help. Freud realized this, and much of his work was based on bringing repressed traumas to the surface. Primal therapy operates on the theory that for many of us birth constitutes a major trauma, and we shall never be fully functioning unless we relive that trauma and let it go. Arthur Janov, who developed primal therapy, believed that pain always stays in the system until it is relived. We have to go through the original pain again in order to be finally free from it.

Until I underwent therapy with Veronica, I would never have thought that I was the kind of person to succumb to obsessive love. Over the years I had persuaded myself that it was all John's fault, that it was entirely because of him that I had suffered so much. The possibility that my one-time obsessive behaviour might constitute a serious, lasting disturbance and disruption had simply never once occurred to me.

As the therapy, which will be described in more detail in Chapter 4, progressed, I began to learn more about obsessive love. I learned that it had prevented me from relating properly to other people, that throughout my adult life I had always been in great fear that it might happen again if I wasn't very careful. So in my relationships I had been pragmatic, controlled, non-passionate, non-emotional. I thought this was how I was − but in some part of myself I had realized that there was something I always held back from full commitment.

I believe now that I was secretly afraid of what might happen if I gave full commitment to a relationship, and so I let the others do all the work. I let them love me and come after me, rather than being active myself. Having gone very badly out of control once, I did not want it to happen again − I did not want to drown in a sea of emotion and passion. So I kept rather uptight, and thought this was part of my personality. Indeed, when Neville heard the tapes after I had been for therapy to release the trauma he said he hadn't realized I had such a passionate nature. It had been dammed up for all of those years − and I had never realized it.

I also learned from Veronica Stephenson that obsessive love always seems to follow a similar pattern. Always, there is the feeling of going out of control, of being unable to act calmly and rationally. Feelings are never returned. Always there is a feeling that one's own identity is gradually being taken away. And always, there is residual hurt which never quite goes away − until the dark secret can somehow be extricated.

In Chapter 2, we will take a look at some other case histories, of both 'ordinary' and famous people, to get a clearer idea of obsessive love in action.

2 Different Kinds of Obsession

Obsessive love is often seen as a slightly more extreme version of falling in love. It is commonly viewed as passion which has got slightly out of hand, but which is really nothing to worry about. Young people suffering the pangs of obsessive or unrequited love are often advised by those purporting to be older and wiser that it is merely a rite of passage, something every teenager has to go through on the way to genuine love. Rarely is it seen as a serious trauma, something deeply and lastingly upsetting. Here are some stories of both 'ordinary' people and extremely famous individuals whose lives have been turned upside down by becoming besotted with a person who does not love them in return.

Olivia's story

Twenty-year-old Olivia was used to attention from boys. She had attended a progressive co-ed boarding school, and by the time she went to university after a year off travelling around India and South America with a girlfriend she felt herself to be perfectly cool and sophisticated. She had lost her virginity at the age of sixteen, and since then had had three other lovers. Her parents had divorced when she was ten and both had now remarried. They were successful lawyers and Olivia had always been used to plenty of money and big houses. She got into Oxford easily, and was enjoying a heady round of socializing and not much work when she met Peter.

Peter had also been at Oxford, but was now working in films

– or sort of working in films. He came from a very rich family and had no real need to work at all. He was handsome, feckless and, to Olivia, extremely attractive. She fell for him from the minute she met him at a party.

She says: 'I thought he was the most wonderful man I had ever met and I could hardly believe it when he asked me out. From then on I just waited for his letters and phone calls. It was agony. Whenever he said he'd ring, he didn't. When he said he'd turn up, he didn't. Then sometimes he'd turn up without warning and I'd cancel everything to be with him.

'He was a wonderful lover and always apologized profusely for being late or not turning up. He would send me flowers and poems, and I was in a state of high excitement all the time.

'I think what I liked about him was that he seemed extremely well-read and well-informed. He'd seen all the films, all the plays, and had views on them all. I knew he wasn't that interested in me, but I loved him so desperately.

'Then, he disappeared – or at least, I couldn't seem to contact him. I couldn't eat, couldn't sleep, and there was never any answer from his phone. I went through agonies, but never mentioned anything to anybody. I started to suffer from anorexia nervosa and my work suffered. My personality seemed to change as well – from being an outgoing, extrovert kind of person I became extremely withdrawn and quiet. All my friends wondered what on earth was wrong – but I couldn't tell them because I felt that they wouldn't understand.

'Then, out of the blue one day, he rang – after about six months. He said he'd been on location, was incredibly apologetic and invited me to his parents' house for dinner. They lived in this amazing huge house in Hampstead and were obviously loaded. But I had the very strong impression that it was all show – like Peter.

'I knew, of course, that he was no good for me, that he had lots of other girls, and that all the poems and flowers meant nothing. But I could not get him out of my mind.

'I haven't seen him for several months now and for him, probably, the relationship is over. The trouble is that all other boys, particularly those of my own age, seem boring and ordinary by comparison.

'It was the anorexia that really brought home to me just what an effect Peter had had. In the summer I was wearing layers of cardigans to keep myself warm, and I became very isolated. I didn't want to speak to anybody else – just to think of Peter all the time. Nothing seemed to matter any more.

'During the summer vacation my mother persuaded me to go to a centre for eating disorders. I was very reluctant. They helped a bit, but I'm still suffering from anorexia. I'm still too thin, I'm still shivering, and I still can't eat properly.

'As a result of what I felt for Peter, I have no interest in relationships any more. Nobody else I have met since means anything to me, and I still yearn for him. I jump when the phone goes, and keep hoping he'll write, that he'll contact me. It's like a kind of addiction, which is why I now think I'm suffering from anorexia. I feel I'm addicted to somebody who is no good for me – and I just can't get over it. I'm just so unhappy. I'd like to find somebody else, but how?'

Pauline's story

Pauline came from a poor family. Extremely talented at art, her parents had wanted her to leave school at sixteen and get a job, but the art master persuaded them to let her stay on and take A-levels and then go to art college. They reluctantly agreed – although nobody in their family had ever had higher education, let alone in something so airy-fairy and non-vocational, as they saw art.

At college, Pauline felt at a distinct disadvantage compared to the other students, who all seemed to have lots of arty clothes, money, exciting friends and fantastic holidays in exotic places. Pauline had to work in a factory in the vacations, just so she had enough money to live on.

One of her lecturers, Martin, thought that Pauline was unusually talented and wanted to encourage her. Her painting flourished under his guidance, but before long she was hopelessly in love with him. Martin was married, with three small children, and had taken only a professional interest in Pauline. But he was flattered by her attentions, and they ended up in bed together.

From then on, Pauline became obsessed with Martin. She would not leave him alone: she hung round his home and started phoning him at all hours. Martin confessed to his wife that he was having an affair with a student, but added that, from his point of view, it was not serious. But Pauline still could not leave him alone. She painted pictures for him, she wrote to him, she declared her undying love for him in letter after letter. Eventually, Martin's wife issued an ultimatum: either you stop seeing this girl, and stop her from pestering us, or I leave you and take the children with me. Martin told Pauline, as kindly as he could, that the affair could not go on, and that, though he was fond of her, he wanted to stay with his wife.

Pauline sobbed that she could not live without him, and the day after this conversation took an overdose. She was admitted to hospital, but would not tell anybody why she had taken an overdose. She decided, though, that she could not carry on at the art college and left at the end of her second year to go to a college near her home. She is now living at home with her parents. She still thinks of Martin, she still tries to phone him at college, and she still writes to him. He never replies, and she spends most of her days in agony.

She feels her life has been ruined – and cannot understand what happened to her. Her mother tells her she will meet somebody else, but somehow she doubts it.

Robert's story

Studying architecture in Scotland, Robert was a long way from home. His parents, although British, lived in Florida and he was able to go home only during the long vacation. He had never really settled down in Scotland, and found it difficult to make close friends.

In his second year he met Marina. She was small, dark and, he thought, wonderfully pretty. He wanted to get to know her, but could not bring himself to ask her out. He thought that if he made sure he was always near her she would soon get the message and realize how interested he was. But she didn't. She flirted, or seemed to flirt, with all the other students, and

Robert felt consumed with jealously. 'However can I attract a wonderful girl like this?' he thought.

Eventually, he bought two tickets for a concert and plucked up courage to ask Marina to accompany him. She refused, saying she had something else on that night, but that it was nice of him to ask. She then ran off, laughing, with a crowd of other boys. Robert felt mortified – but even more mortified when he went to the concert alone, having turned in the other ticket, and saw Marina there with a boyfriend. She was obviously enjoying herself. She waved airily at him, smiling. Robert could not stand it, and did not return to the concert after the interval.

He could not get Marina out of his mind. She clearly wasn't interested and did not seem to realize that he was absolutely besotted. His work suffered, and he failed his second year exams. Robert decided not to resit them and so his intended career as an architect was at an end – but he felt there was no way he could continue to be at the same university as Marina. He could not bear to see her with other boys, having a good time, while he was consumed with misery.

Three typical stories – all of students. All had fallen hopelessly in love, and seemed powerless to prevent the misery and longing that resulted from their unrequited passions. An anonymous teenager writing in the *Guardian* in 1990 well describes the ups and downs, the wild swings of love and hate, the self-loathing and the confusion which beset young people when they fall desperately and miserably in love:

My heartbeat went up so high that I nearly fainted ... I never believed all that stuff about blood pressure going up when you see someone you love, but honestly my blood pressure went up so high that I could hardly speak. I'm still hot and excited now; just thinking of him makes me want to cry.

Maybe it isn't love, but you know, I'm pretty sure it is. I still haven't got over the hurt he caused me. But I just can't stop loving him. The thing that hurts me most is knowing that he hates me. Maybe sometime in the future we have hope. Nobody understands how I feel. They say I am only a child and don't understand love. That's their excuse. A child has feelings as well. I love him. If only he knew how strongly I feel about him.

I don't understand why he hates me. It's probably because I'm so ugly and fat. Mum says I'm pretty and have a nice figure but if that's true why does he hate me? Why do boys hate me? He's so gorgeous!... I love him for how he is and nothing else. I have tried to forget him and like other boys but it's hard and always when it comes to the crunch I still love him. I've tried to hate him but I can't. He'll always be in my heart.

He hates me. Why do I torture myself writing it? I didn't think love could cause so much pain. Seeing him chat up all the other girls and then slagging me off. You know, I never thought he'd do it to my face ... The tears I've cried over him could fill the Atlantic Ocean ... I've been so moody lately and my parents have noticed it and want to know what's going on ... I really want to tell them but they'll just say it's a part of growing up and shrug it off. They don't understand ...

This lament probably echoes the feelings of all young people who have ever loved and not felt confident that their love is returned. There is the feeling that nobody understands, a sense of complete isolation and inability to share this misery with anybody else, or to overcome it in any way.

But although obsessive, unrequited love may be for many people an aspect of growing up, it is by no means confined to the young, or to first or early loves.

Gaynor's story

After qualifying as a pharmacist, Gaynor worked for a few years in this profession, but then grew bored and wanted a different kind of challenge. She got a job working in the PR department of an international pharmaceuticals company. It was a far more exciting job than her previous one, and offered many opportunities for travel. She also met many more people than when she was working in a lab.

At twenty-eight she was still single, though secretly hoping to meet somebody who would 'take her away from all this'. Then, at an international conference, she met Richard. He was a medical journalist working on a prestigious daily newspaper and she thought he was the most handsome man she had ever seen.

She was told that he had a bad reputation with women, but was nevertheless flattered when he knocked on the door of her hotel room one night. They made love – and Gaynor fell in love. She became besotted with Richard, for whom the affair was simply a one-night stand: he was not particularly attracted to her and had no intention of repeating the incident.

Back home, however, she could not forget him. She phoned him up at his newspaper, invited him out to lunch on the pretext of giving him a story, lived in hope of seeing him, being with him. But he paid her no attention.

Eventually, heartbroken, Gaynor formed a relationship with a chap she met through work and who, like her, was working in medical PR. She could not love him, but was still longing to 'settle down'. They bought a house together, had two children and set up a PR company together. On the surface, all looks fine – Gaynor and Bill work together, take turns looking after the children and have a thriving business.

But Gaynor, now thirty-eight, feels that she cannot stand living with Bill for much longer. He is simply not Richard; he is not exciting, he is not handsome – and she still can't get Richard out of her mind. What makes it worse is that not long after Gaynor met him, Richard left his wife and began living with a glamorous fellow journalist on the same paper. Gaynor now feels plain, rejected, miserable – and says that not a day goes by when she doesn't yearn for Richard, even though she knows he treated her badly.

'How can I get him out of my mind?' she wonders.

Annabel's story

In her thirties and married with two small children, one day Annabel met David, who was also married with one child. She met him through her husband's work as a hospital doctor, and the two families soon became good friends. Annabel had given up her exciting job in an advertising agency when the children came along, and was now rather bored with life. She was considering going back to work, possibly part-time, but after eight years, felt she would have completely lost touch and she had also lost confidence in herself as a career woman.

She was, though, immensely attractive and lively. She had long ago ceased to love Andrew, her husband, and increasingly wondered whatever she had seen in him. She had married him because he had seemed kind and reliable, in complete contrast to her father, who was addicted to gambling. But David, although in the same profession as Andrew, was different.

For one thing, he was six foot four and had a brooding, melancholy kind of face. He looked as if he would climb the ladder quickly, and in fact he soon became a consultant gynaecologist. He was also, it was obvious, attracted to Annabel. Secretly they began an affair, and Annabel fell deeply in love with David. She could not stop thinking about him night and day, but at the same time as finding him overwhelmingly attractive she felt slightly frightened by him. He could flare up and be angry – violent, even.

Annabel viewed his moods and his silences as frustration that they could not be together all the time, that they were joined to other partners. But always she felt that her love for David was stronger than his love for her. In the end, however, her obsession gave her the strength to tell Andrew she wanted to leave him, and there was an extremely bitter divorce. She married David, and the two of them set up home not far from their previous homes. David's wife was shattered, and forbade him access to their daughter.

When confronted with the reality of living together, the obsession petered out. After eight years the relationship has soured and love has gone. Annabel now wants to divorce David, but feels uneasy about having two failed marriages. Also, after putting all her energies into falling in love and setting up home with David she still does not have a career; she feels her hopes of being financially self-sufficient are slimmer now than ever.

The overwhelming love she had for David has turned to hate. She feels she fell in love with an illusion, with a fantasy, rather than the real man. When she got to know the real man, she didn't like him so much. She feels that David has since shown himself in his true colours — but she has become so dependent on him that she doesn't know how to leave him and lead her own life. She is in despair.

Those on the 'other side'

Of course, in every story of obsessive love there are two people involved — the one who is so hopelessly in love, and the one on the receiving end. Endless poems, stories, plays and novels, have depicted these people as being cruel, heartless, ruthless amoral, scheming and with no feelings at all for the poor helpless individuals who have had the misfortune to fall in love with them.

But are they really always like that? What is it actually like to be on the receiving end of somebody's obsessive love? The following two stories show that it may not be at all comfortable — in fact can be frightening and bewildering — to be the loved, rather than the loving, one.

Adam's story

To his friends, Adam seemed to be an exciting, witty and highly entertaining companion. He had trained as an actor, but after a few years when he spent more time resting than working, he decided to go to university as a mature student to read English and drama. While there he started to write plays, which were put on by the university dramatic society.

At the time, Adam was thirty and single. He had never wanted to get married, and all his previous affairs had been brief and unsatisfactory. But one by one all his friends seemed to be marrying and having families, and Adam began to feel lonely, as if he was missing out. He particularly longed to have a child.

Rebecca was another mature student, also thirty when she met Adam. She had been teaching in a secondary school for several years, but wanted a change and so enrolled on a Women's Studies MA course. She was also interested in drama and literature, and soon after meeting Adam fell desperately in love with him.

He says: 'She was so hopelessly in love with me, though I just couldn't feel anything for her. But wherever I went, there was Rebecca. She had been briefly married before, but not happily. I suppose I was flattered by her attentions, and I also felt sorry for her. I wished I could love her, return the strength of feelings, but I couldn't.

'However, we became close, we exchanged confidences, and eventually started to live together.' After both finished their courses, they got married. Adam was then thirty-five and his longing to have a child was greater than ever, but Rebecca stalled. Eventually she changed her mind, and three years later they had a daughter.

Rebecca was now back teaching in a different school, and Adam was struggling to make a living as a playwright. Now aged forty-three he and Rebecca are divorced. He says: 'I can't really understand it. She was so obsessed with me, it seemed as if she had to have me at any price. Then, not long after our daughter Ingrid was born, she seemed to change.

'She accused me of not being a proper provider, of making her go back to work before she was ready, and of remaining a perpetual adolescent. She also said that I had never really loved her, that I always spoke to her as if I was speaking lines, and that I was not a proper feeling person.

'Her love had turned to hate, and now that we are divorced she simply won't speak to me unless she has to. She still has strong feelings towards me – but it's as if she has flipped the coin. I feel guilty for never being able to love her in the way she loved me – but now I wonder whether it *was* love. At times I felt as if she was smothering me, trying to take me over.'

Neither Rebecca nor Adam has remarried, and Adam feels that Rebecca never will. He feels certain that, in spite of everything that has happened, Rebecca would have him back – under certain conditions. 'But there's no way that I would want to live with her again,' he said. 'She seemed to want to keep me in her pocket, and never even wanted us to go out together. She seemed to want me all to herself — and didn't even want a child to come between us.

'Yet when she had Ingrid she became surprisingly maternal. I can't understand it at all.'

Brigid's story

When Hans entered her life Brigid was forty-six, divorced and the mother of two grown-up children. He was fifty, a highly successful international businessman, and also divorced.

Brigid, who works as a cancer counsellor, says: 'You end up horribly confused. It seems that whatever you do, there's nothing that minimizes the obsession. When I first realized Hans was interested, I could hardly believe it. After all, I was nobody really, and he was this highly educated, well-travelled, well-spoken, sophisticated man. I wasn't young, I wasn't beautiful, I didn't have any money.

'He was an interesting person, extremely intelligent and very attractive. For about three months after he met me he took me out to dinner, sent me flowers and was the perfect gentleman. He did not try to seduce me, or get me to live with him or marry him.

'Then one day he asked me to go to Holland, his native country, with him for the weekend. I refused at first, but he said: "Surely you can trust me." I thought: "Well, he's never tried to get me into bed or anything." So I went. We went by boat, and he showed me into my cabin. It was huge, and my heart sank. So this is it, I thought, he's conned me.

'He must have read my thoughts because he said: "No, this is *your* room. Mine's down the corridor." Then I began to trust him again. We had dinner together, and he showed me to my room. He came in, saying that he wouldn't touch me, wouldn't bother me if I didn't want him to.

'Of course, we did end up sleeping together — and he was the most wonderful lover I had ever had. We never lived together, but after we got back he was on the phone every other day. He kept saying: "You'll never lose me."

'I realized after a time that he was completely obsessed. I became very confused and tried to leave him several times, but always he pleaded with me to go back to him. He professed undying love to me, and I never doubted that he did love me, although it certainly didn't *feel* like love. It was something strange and I couldn't understand it.

'Throughout the three years we eventually spent together, things never became normal. Sometimes he wouldn't speak to me – he was very moody – and then he would become ridiculously attentive and ask me to forgive him.

'The funny thing,' Brigid says, 'was that he wasn't obsessively jealous. He liked to show me off to other men, was pleased if other men were attracted to me. But he wanted to control me. He said, that if he could lock me up and keep me to himself, he would. He kept saying: "You belong to me." It was as if I wasn't a separate person at all.

'It all ended very badly. I simply could not cope with him, and said I had had enough. He then threatened me and I got scared, as I live alone. One day, at work, I discovered my car had been tampered with, and I knew it was him.

'The doctor for whom I work called the police, and Hans was arrested. I got an injunction for him not to molest me and he was put in a cell for a few hours. He didn't contact me at all for the length of time the injunction lasted, but then started writing letters again.

'I felt sorry for him and felt guilty for hurting him. I started worrying about what he was going through, the agony he must be facing. I saw him once or twice after that, but told him that on no account was I going back to him.

'But just recently I got a phone call from him to say that he was in hospital with cancer. I went to see him and arranged care for him, but wouldn't go back. As a cancer counsellor it's what I'd do for anybody, but of course I feel horribly guilty that he's got cancer because of his obsession with me, and that his illness is a way of punishing me.

'When I asked him whatever attracted him to me, he said: "It's your voice." I also believe that, because I work as a counsellor, he saw me as having a sympathetic manner. Perhaps he saw me as a mother figure – he had lost his own mother at a very early age."

These are all stories of 'ordinary' people, those, who, without ever really wanting it, have been caught in the grip of a passion they don't really understand and which certainly does not make them happy or fulfilled. Instead, their love has caused endless frustration, fear and discomfort. There is never, it seems, a 'marriage of true minds', never genuine companionship, but always an overwhelming longing on the part of the lover, and at best feelings of guilt, at worst feelings of indifference, on the party of the beloved. There is never a comfortable feeling, never any real rapport.

As Brigid said, to those on the receiving end it never feels like love, even though the 'victims' may not doubt the sincerity and the genuineness of the emotions of those who are besotted.

Famous cases of obsessive love

Obsessive love has, as we have seen, been one of the favourite themes of creative writers. But it often also hits creative people, those who are destined to become great writers or poets. And thanks to their works we can discover exactly what obsessive love feels like, whether or not we have experienced it ourselves.

Charlotte Brontë

One of the most famous 'real life' cases was that of Charlotte Brontë, who fell desperately in love with her teacher, Constantin Heger, while she was studying with her sister Emily in Brussels. At the time both Charlotte and Emily were 'mature students', being in their mid-twenties, and the idea was that they should gain further 'accomplishments' to enable them to set up their own school in their father's parsonage at Haworth in Yorkshire.

In the event Emily fled back home after a year, leaving the more adventurous and robust Charlotte to study alone, and to fall ever more deeply in love with the Professor, who taught at the school run by his wife, Zoë. Madame Heger soon realized what was going on, and although she probably did not seriously believe her husband would succumb to Charlotte's passionate love, or even commit adultery, she gradually withdrew what

31

had been the high point of Charlotte's life at the Pensionnat – her weekly English lessons with the Professor.

When the Hegers went for their annual holiday and Charlotte was left more or less alone at the Pensionnat she broke down completely, being unable to eat or sleep. In her extremity she sought out a Catholic priest – like most Protestants of the time, she had a horror of anything 'Romish' or 'Popish' – but who else was there? She went to the Cathedral of St Gudule and walked into a confessional box. But the confession – if indeed Charlotte did confess her 'illicit' love for a married man – seemed to do her little good.

She returned home to Haworth on New Year's Day 1844. Then her real anguish began, painfully described in her novel *Villette*, in which Lucy Snowe falls for the intriguing teacher Paul Emanuel.

Charlotte began to write passionately to her former teacher, and waited for the postman to bring her the longed-for letters from Heger. At first he did send some hastily scribbled notes in return, but then possibly became nervous of the intensity and ardour of his strange pupil's missives and did not bother to reply further. He had already told her that, if she did write, the content of her letters should be confined to family and neutral matters. Perhaps he too suspected that his gifted pupil harboured feelings for him which did not properly belong to a pupil-teacher relationship.

When Charlotte's letters became more obvious declarations of anguished love it seems that he simply screwed them up and put them in the wastepaper basket, hardly reading them. They were retrieved and kept by Madame Heger, who possibly sensed that Charlotte was some kind of genius and that the letters might some day be worth something. Now, of course, they are priceless.

In one letter, carefully preserved by Zoë Heger, Charlotte threw caution to the winds and wrote: 'Day and night I can find neither rest nor peace. If I sleep I am disturbed by tormenting dreams in which I see you always severe, always grave, always incensed against me.' Even this did not bring forth a reply, and gradually Charlotte realized the situation was hopeless. She appeared to get over her suffering eventually and married her father's curate, Arthur Bell Nicholls. She also became one of the leading women novelists of her day; *Jane Eyre* was an instant bestseller.

There have been very many biographies of Charlotte Brontë – her life at Haworth continues to attract – but it seems to me that many biographers and Brontë enthusiasts have not given due weight to Charlotte's obsession for Heger, which fits into the classic mould. Of course, she had many other sorrows to cope with – the death of her brother and two sisters, and a very late first pregnancy at the age of thirty-eight not long after she married Nicholls. But I feel certain that the obsession with Heger left a deep and abiding trauma which hastened her death.

Elizabeth Smart

The author of *By Grand Central Station I Sat Down and Wept* was for many years passionately in love with the poet George Barker, by whom she eventually had four children. Born into a diplomat's family in 1913, Elizabeth Smart was brought up to lead a life of leisure but always harboured a desire to become a writer. She actually fell in love with Barker before meeting him, when she read some of his poems in London. Barker, at twenty-seven the same age as Elizabeth, was already a published poet and at the time a professor in Japan. He wanted to leave this job, and thanks to Smart's connections was enabled to come to America.

There was one serious problem – he was already married. Even so, within a month of meeting they were already lovers and soon Smart became pregnant with Barker's child. Her diaries, published in 1990 as *Necessary Secrets*, chronicle the progress of her love affair with him.

As in most (all?) cases of obsessive love, Barker did not return the passion, although he was clearly fond of his besotted and attractive, well-connected lover. But he kept returning to his wife Jessica, which aroused Smart's uncontrollable jealousy.

In one terrible passage in her diaries (which also appears in slightly altered form in *By Grand Central Station*), she writes:

Perhaps I am his hope. But she is his present. And if then she is his present, I am not his present. Therefore I am not,

33

and I wonder why no one has noticed I am dead and taken the trouble to bury me. My utter collapse cannot even bother to do the clear deed of death but cringes glazed or weeps a tear of sheer weakness.

He is not with me because he is sleeping with her. That is the barrier to any abandonment to love.

Why does he say minor martyrdoms? Didn't the crucifixion last only three days? Is it the shortness of the days of torture or the fact that hope still breathes that lets him say minor? How can anything so total not be major? He has martyred me but for no cause nor has he any idea of the size or consequence of my wounds.

I read Troilus and Cressida *and other tales of love. But the very word I avoid. Until I have it in my very arms and I will have nothing else, the world and all others are blank, and the days airless regions boggling even astronomers.*

Kathleen Raine

The poet Kathleen Raine's story provides further confirmation that you do not have to be young to suffer from obsession. She was nearly forty when she fell in love with the aristocratic adventurer Gavin Maxwell, author of *Ring of Bright Water*.

Kathleen Raine met Maxwell when recovering from a nervous breakdown and two failed marriages. She thought he looked like a 'blind bird' − he always wore dark glasses − and was certain that the meeting, which took place at a friend's flat in London, was heaven-sent. She was not, she said in *The Lion's Mouth*, her account of the affair, looking for a lover, and Gavin was never to be her lover. She hoped that 'what was between us was something else altogether'. She was convinced they had been brother and sister in some previous life, so close did she feel the affinity between them to be.

The trouble was, Maxwell did not share this conviction. At first he found Kathleen useful, but then grew tired of her. 'I loved Gavin with my whole soul,' Kathleen wrote − but he was indifferent in return. He was basically homosexual, and from the first told Kathleen that no physical consummation could be considered.

Kathleen wanted to be indispensable to Gavin, so that he could not live without her. Once, when he brought a friend to stay with him at his Scottish island of Sandaig while Kathleen was there, she felt excluded and ignored. In terrible despair, she cursed him under his favourite rowan tree. She wrote:

Weeping, I laid my hands upon the trunk, calling upon the tree for justice; let Gavin suffer in this place, as I am suffering now. I was at that moment beside myself as one-pointed and as blazingly clear as a streak of lightning as I spoke aloud my terrible invocation. And I went up the hill to Mary and John Donald [neighbours] with the dagger of anguish churning in my heart.

A couple of days later her terrible grief had died down, but she had the very strong feeling that she had set in motion a chain of events which could not be reversed. Gavin Maxwell certainly thought so. On reading the manuscript of *The Lion's Mouth* he came across the curse, and blamed it for the fact that his life had never gone right since she uttered it. Seven years after that curse, he was dead of cancer.

Kathleen Raine wrote in the book that since her involvement with Gavin she had never taken another lover, but had spent every night alone since she stayed one night with him, albeit chastely. Later, after she had been responsible for the death of his famous otter Mijbil while she was supposed to be looking after the animal at Sandaig, she felt that Gavin completely shut his heart to her.

For a long time afterwards, if anybody ever asked her whether she knew Gavin Maxwell she would say no. Maxwell certainly never publicly acknowledged any relationship with Kathleen Raine, except to refer to her as the 'poetess' who put a curse on him. In *Raven Seek Thy Brother* he wrote that he could not understand what must have been going through her mind.

Three famous writers – three famous obsessions with charismatic, attractive and unusual men, one-sided love affairs which caused the women far more agony and anguish than happiness. In fact, the moments of happiness with their lovers for each were few – the moments of despair and desolation frequent.

Carrington

A slightly different case of obsessive love is that of the painter Dora Carrington (always known only by her surname) for the writer Lytton Strachey, both members of the Bloomsbury group. Strachey, a self-confessed homosexual, fell in love with Ralph Partridge, a young writer. In order to be near Strachey Carrington married Partridge, and for several years the three maintained a strange *ménage à trois*.

Carrington was rather butch in appearance, and said on more than one occasion that she did not like sex. Her marriage to Partridge was most probably celibate – at least for most of its duration. Strachey was probably attracted to her boyishness, and it was when he apparently made a pass at her that Carrington succumbed. She remained hopelessly in love with Strachey, and when he died could not bear to go on living. Some weeks after his death she shot herself, and died not long after.

Ruth Ellis

The last woman to be hanged in Britain died for her obsessive love of David Blakely, a handsome, drunken, upper-class wastrel she met in the after-hours drinking club where she was a manageress.

At the time, Ruth was in her mid-twenties and had two children by different men. She was married to an alcoholic doctor, but by this time rarely saw him. Blakely, at twenty-three, was a couple of years younger, and for Ruth it was love at first sight.

The end of the affair is well known. At the Magdala pub in Hampstead, on Easter Sunday, 11 April, 1955, Ruth Ellis – crazed with obsessive love, with the trauma of a recent abortion, and with drink and pills – pumped six bullets into David Blakely.

Blakely, like so many young men who dimly realize they are objects of some kind of obsession, had tried to wriggle out of the affair with Ruth. He had other women, and kept breaking it off and then wanting to see her again. Also, like so many young men, he was sexually attracted to this slim peroxide blonde who, though from a working-class family, gave herself airs and tried to speak 'posh'.

Until the day she died Ruth's obsession with David never dimmed, but at her trial, when she was asked if she loved him 'so very much', she replied, 'No, not really' — the words that, more than anything else that she said or did, condemned her. It seems that after she killed David Ruth did not want to live. Although he had been such a very unsatisfactory lover, she could never get him out of her mind. Her mad drinking was probably an attempt to tranquillize herself, to anaesthetize the feelings she had for him but which would never be returned.

It may seem, from the stories so far, that women are more likely than men to fall obsessively in love. This is very probably the case, for reasons that will be discussed in the following chapters. But men too can fall prey to uncontrollable passions, as Brigid's case history shows.

One of the most famous examples of male obsessive love is that of the Prince of Wales, later Edward VIII, for the twice-divorced Mrs Wallis Simpson. When she met the Prince Wallis was neither young nor beautiful, although she was extremely stylish and gamine in appearance. In addition she was also American and a commoner. It was not a suitable match at all, but the Prince was determined to have her. According to the latest biography, by Philip Ziegler, the Duke of Windsor remained so obsessively in love with Wallis for the whole thirty-four years of their marriage that his eyes would follow her round the room and he would become distressed and upset if she was not with him for even a day.

For Edward, there was simply no choice in the matter. Whatever the cost — even that of giving up the throne — it was of little consequence compared with his determination to have the woman of his dreams.

Whenever there is obsessive love, reason, rationality and logic fly out of the window. But why? Why do so many of us torture ourselves by loving those who can't reciprocate, who are not interested, who are unavailable, who are homosexual, married, out of reach — or individuals who are, by any reasonable and rational assessment, completely unsuitable? What is it that makes us fall for people who cannot make us happy, but cause us only despair and anguish — even though they

37

may not do so deliberately? It all seems very strange – and mysterious.

Chapter 3 will look at some of the factors which may predispose some people to fall obsessively – and often dangerously – in love, when that love is not requited.

3 Causes and Effects

Obsessive love appears to be a highly destructive passion which seems to have no real purpose or happy end result. Certainly it is rarely life-enhancing or uplifting for those caught in its grip. But how do these obsessive feelings arise in the first place? Why are they so very strong? Why can't we control them? The answers will, I hope, shed some light for those who have ever been obsessively in love, and also for those who are wrestling with such feelings now.

Types of obsession

The word 'obsession' is often used rather loosely in our language and has, in some cases, come to mean simply a strong liking for something. We may say that somebody is 'absolutely obsessed' with football or tennis, or with collecting pictures of Princess Diana. Indeed, when schoolgirls are asked to list their hobbies they often mention 'Princess Diana' as a hobby in itself, and they may say they are 'obsessed' with her when all they mean is that they have an abiding interest in the glamorous wife of Britain's future king.

'Obsession' is also the name of a modern American perfume, and clearly the manufacturers must have thought there was something good about the word. After all, it is highly unlikely that they would have named an expensive perfume 'Paranoia' or 'Psychosis' − both of which states can accompany obsessive love.

It is important, I think, to distinguish between various types of obsession, not all of which may have any connection with obsessive love. In the first place, there are those people who are so obsessive about their hobby or interest that it becomes the most important thing in their life; in some cases, the only important thing. There are the 'twitchers', those super-dedicated birdwatchers who will plan amazingly complicated and expensive journeys just to see a particular bird sitting on a branch in Scotland, for instance. Twitchers have highly organized networks, so that they can relay information about rare birds to each other instantly – and sighting specific birds is more important to them than anything else. Since the advent of personal computers many people have become completely obsessive about computerizing everything, and can lose all sense of time and place when sitting at their machines. Other people may become obsessed by jogging, exercise, sailing or some other sport, so that they live for the times they are carrying out these activities.

There is also the very distressing obsessive-compulsive disorder, whose sufferers have to keep washing their hands, checking that the electric light is off, or enacting a series of highly complicated rituals before leaving the house. In some cases, OCD gets so bad that sufferers cannot even leave their homes – the rituals that they must do each day, such as touching the arm of a particular chair and walking four paces to the right, then to the left, become so time-consuming that they take up too many hours of the day.

There are the 'superfans', those who are so obsessed about a particular pop or film star that they decorate their homes with posters and memorabilia of the admired one, and spend all their money following them around, attending every concert or show that they possibly can. And there are people who are obsessed with the British royal family to the extent that they will try to gain access to their houses, and even their bedrooms.

But while all these aberrations may be of interest to the psychologist, the phenomenon of passionate, unrequited love for somebody who, theoretically at least, might be able to return the affection is the most fascinating and mysterious of all obsessions.

Twitchers and computer freaks are often extreme introverts – dull, silent people who find it difficult to communicate with the outside world. Those suffering from obsessive-compulsive disorder have a severe mental health problem, caused, it is believed, by extreme anxiety. Again, sufferers from OCD are often shrinking violets, nervous, timid people who subconsciously complicate their lives with meaningless rituals so that they do not have to venture into the outside world or take responsibility for themselves. The 'superfans', and those obsessed by members of the royal family, people whom they are never likely to meet or have any kind of real relationship with, are, I believe, individuals who substitute this kind of unreal relationship for a genuine one. Rather than try to find somebody they can properly relate to, they put all their energies into fantasy relationshps.

By contrast, many people who fall obsessively in love are extrovert, bold, colourful, ambitious characters who are actually capable of making good, reciprocal and equal relationships – but find their lives unaccountably sabotaged, often for years or decades, because of their peculiar, unrequited passion for one particular person. Whereas dedicated hobbyists might be 'obsessive' people generally, the kind whom Freud described as anally fixated, and whereas sufferers from OCD have a definable disorder, those obsessively in love often seem quite normal – that is, until the overwhelming passion hits them.

Is obsessive love some kind of mental disorder?

Clearly, for the time that obsessive love is at its height it is not a normal state of being. There is an overwhelming feeling of being taken over, of being invaded by an alien, so that you seem compelled to act in all kinds of uncharacteristic and possibly self-destructive ways. There seems no choice in the matter.

You have to follow and pursue the beloved, and there seems no way you can help yourself. And nothing makes any difference, not even the most cold and forbidding behaviour on the part of the beloved. It doesn't matter how callous and uncaring that person is, or what he or she does to try to minimize the obsession. The passion continues unabated until it eventually goes underground, wears itself out or, in some extreme cases, ends in violence.

41

Usually, however, obsessive love is an episode in the lives of sufferers rather than being a chronic condition. There has usually been no indication of psychiatric disturbance before, and there may well not be again, although obsessive love can sometimes lead to disturbed behaviour or breakdowns.

And usually it is one particular person who sparks off the obsession. Some people always seem to be obsessed with one person after another, but these are not obsessive lovers as the book understands them (though they too are suffering from a chronic psychiatric disturbance). 'True' obsessive lovers rarely experience this kind of grand passion more than once, or with more than one person.

The lack of response on the part of the 'victim' is also, I believe, a significant factor in the development of obsessive feelings. The feelings arise unbidden, it is true, and from then on it becomes extremely difficult to damp them down. But the very fact of the lack of reciprocity appears to give these feelings what they need to feed on.

One abiding characteristic of obsessive love is that the object of the affection is always somebody who is, for some reason, unavailable. This happens either because of indifference, because the beloved has a different sexual orientation, is married, or is simply not interested in a lasting relationship. It is the very unavailability of these characters − who nevertheless always have 'something' about them − which seems to feed the obsession.

Because there is no response, or at least, not the response that is ardently desired, the obsessive lover has to live in a world of combined agony and make-believe, where he or she lives for the moments when the beloved will be seen, or when there will be some kind of exchange. In the meantime, fancies and fantasies take over.

In bed, at night, the obsessed lover will fantasize having the beloved there. In fact, the fantasy may be more attractive than the reality − at least in fantasy the lover can be always clean, always ardent, always responsive, which even the most attractive and desirable 'real person' cannot.

But although obsessive love may be some kind of aberration, it seems overwhelmingly likely that it is something which can affect anybody at all, however sane and rational and pragmatic and analytical they may be otherwise. Nobody can guard against it – which is why it cannot be classed as an aspect of mental illness.

Obsessive love has been very little studied by psychiatrists, except for rare cases of those chronically obsessed. In these cases, the obsession is more likely to be a manifestation of some underlying serious disturbance than simply an overwhelming desire to be with a particular person all the time.

The reason, I feel, that the subject has not been seriously addressed by psychiatrists is because it is something that happens to very many 'normal' people, and because very few who have ever suffered in this way would ever consider seeing a psychiatrist. It seems so much a part of normal, ordinary life that it is hardly viewed as strange. It is, in fact, an aspect of the human condition, and so many poets and novelists have written about it that it may appear perfectly ordinary. But its very ordinariness and universality do not mean that obsessive love is good or healthy – or that it can't be healed.

Obsession – or infatuation?

Obsessive love clearly has something in common with infatuation, or crushes. But is it a difference of degree or a difference in kind?

Infatuations and crushes are a mild and relatively harmless form of obsession, which are usually short-lasting. Many teenagers festoon their rooms with posters of their current heroes. But if you ask them a couple of years later about these stars they will most likely have forgotten all about them, or be ashamed that they ever liked them. It is also extremely common for teenagers and pre-teens of both sexes to have crushes on older pupils at school, on teachers of the same or opposite sex, or anybody in some kind of authority role – anybody who seems to have that little bit more wisdom and confidence. Of course, student – teacher, and pupil – guru obsessions are extremely common, as are cases of patients falling desperately in love with their doctors or therapists.

The reasons for all these crushes and obsessions, are, I think, quite clear. When you are a pupil or a patient you are in a relatively weak and vulnerable position, in contrast to the teacher or therapist who may seem wise, all-knowing, guru-like. This 'wise' teacher or doctor may appear to be somebody who knows everything, who can impart wonderful information, or who possesses the power to make you better. Freud recognized that patients frequently fall in love with their therapists, but he called this activity 'transference', meaning that the patient sees the therapist as a parent or lover figure, and transfers the strong affections − or feelings of hate − to the neutral therapist.

But as American psychiatrist Dr Peter Rutter points out in his book *Sex in the Forbidden Zone*, doctors, therapists, lawyers and others in positions of authority and power should be very careful not to abuse this situation to enter into sexual relations with their besotted patients or pupils. Therapists and teachers, he argued, should realize how easy it is to fall desperately in love with those who seem to be wiser and more adult than we are ourselves, and who seem to have tapped some fount of wisdom to which we have not yet gained access.

For this same reason, very many religious gurus inspire a kind of hero-worship in their followers which may border in some cases on obsessive love. It is extremely common for elderly gurus or charismatic leaders to surround themselves with adoring young women who are only too ready to worship and even sleep with this person, who seems so extraordinary and above the ordinary run of humanity. The late Bhagwan Shree Rajneesh reputedly had sex with hundreds of his young female disciples in his heyday during the 1970s. Swami Muktananda, who founded the Siddha Yoga movement, apparently did likewise. One follower of Muktananda even said she would like to drink his urine!

Although such gurus and cult leaders are commonly accused of brainwashing their susceptible disciples, the fact is that the young women who flock round them do so of their own accord. They may even fight for the privilege of spending a night with the beloved one.

The elderly Gandhi, toothless and emaciated, used to sleep (chastely, we are told) with young women. Mass murderer Charles Manson attracted round him a band of adoring, obsessed young women, the women who made up his 'family'.

The good and the wicked alike seem to have this power to attract, but one thing seems constant, whether you call the attraction infatuation, a crush or an obsession, depending on its strength: all the people who inspire this kind of reaction have something over and above the ordinary – at least for the obsessed or infatuated one.

In every case, the 'beloved' person is more powerful, more charismatic, older, more authoritative, wiser, more knowledgeable than the one who is attracted. Whenever there is obsession, a crush or an infatuation, there is never equality. And that is one of the differences between 'real' love and its counterfeit coin, obsession.

Are women more likely than men to become obsessed?

It is noticeable that it is almost always young women who become obsessed by older, more charismatic or powerful men. The opposite hardly ever seems to happen. Whenever a man becomes obsessed, it is usually with a woman or girl much younger and much less powerful than himself.

The nineteenth-century essayist William Hazlitt describes his obsession with a chambermaid; the pre-Raphaelite painters were obsessed with working-class girls and longed to paint them; King Cophetua was beguiled by the beggar-maid, and Edward VIII with Mrs Simpson, who was certainly not at his social level and was a foreigner in addition. The extreme example of course is the 'Lolita' syndrome, described by Vladimir Nabokov. It would be hard to imagine a middle-aged woman becoming so very obsessed with a teenage boy.

What causes people to fall obsessively in love?

Two conditions need to be present when people succumb to obsessive love – time and a certain level of education. (Obsessive love is unknown in pre-literate societies, and it feeds on the kind of romantic notions that are found in certain kinds of fiction.) Given these two factors, there is hardly anybody who cannot fall prey to the passion.

Whatever else it may be, obsessive love is entirely self-generated. Usually the 'beloved', the 'victim', does nothing to bring about the crazy feelings, and may even do all he or she can to stop them – usually without success. We have seen that poets, painters and novelists – creative people – seem particularly prone to falling obsessively in love. Do you, then, have to be more creative, or to have a more vivid imagination, than ordinary people?

No. I think we perhaps imagine that it is more likely to affect highly creative or imaginative people, simply because they are better than most of us at depicting the agonies involved and have a greater gift than inarticulate people for bringing their feelings vividly alive. It may be helpful here to consider the analogy with alcohol. Because so very many highly talented writers have also been alcoholics, it is tempting to believe that alcohol in itself somehow confers or releases creative talent. The love affair that so many writers have had with alcohol has also given intoxicating liquor a kind of dark and raffish glamour. Yet, as we all know, alcohol is a depressant of the central nervous system which eventually adversely affects all those who over-indulge, and actually destroys, rather than enhances, their talents.

In the same way, because so many writers have anguished over their own or their characters' obsessive passions, we may imagine that these overwhelming and uncontrollable feelings are not only confined to genius, but are actually part of it. But the reason that so many writers have struggled with obsessive love is precisely *because* it is dysfunctional, because it is destructive, and because it contaminates rather than uplifts.

Literature basically depicts dysfunction rather than ideal behaviour. In fact, that is the purpose of literature – to try to make sense of passions and feelings which seem inexplicable. This applies not only to great literature, but to popular fiction as well. Psychology attempts to do the same. But because it tends to be written in dry, unapproachable language it does not have the appeal of emotive literature.

But can you think of a hero or heroine whose life was ultimately enhanced by an obsessive, unrequited passion? In every case, such passions end in some kind of tragedy. The real problem, of course, is that obsessive love has come to be seen as some aspect of love, when in reality it is anything but.

Several factors create a climate for obsessive love:

1. Leisure
2. Education
3. Feeling vulnerable and not belonging
4. Having an unjustifiably inflated opinion of oneself
5. Having particular childhood experiences
6. Always feeling 'special' and 'different'
7. Some kind of perceived or real, and unbridgeable, inequality between the lover and the beloved.

Although singly these factors may not cause obsessive feelings to develop, when they come together – wow! When all are present, it would be extremely unlikely if obsessive love did *not* result.

Leisure

In many, if not most, cases, those who fall obsessively in love do not have enough to do. Several of the stories in Chapter 2 were of university students reading arts subjects, which notoriously leave acres of space in the timetable to be filled according to the individual's liking.

In the famous cases Charlotte Brontë, Elizabeth Smart, Kathleen Raine and the Duke of Windsor were all people with plenty of time on their hands – people who had more leisure than they really knew what to do with – and no secure position in the world. Even Ruth Ellis, as manageress of a drinking club, had very many idle hours to fill. What better than to occupy these hours with a hopeless love affair? It seems that obsessive love is like the work that the devil finds for idle hands to do. Or, in this case, idle minds to do.

Anthropologist Branko Bokun, who has studied cultures in many parts of the world, has come to the conclusion that obsessive love almost always happens at times in a person's life when they haven't got enough to do. If you're kept busy, he says, there just isn't time for this kind of feeling to develop.

It is also noticeable that nobody in the case histories was an artisan, somebody who worked with their hands. All worked with their minds. It seems that people who are extremely busy, who labour with their hands rather than with their minds or emotions, are more solidly 'earthed'. Their imaginations don't run riot and they are far less likely than intellectuals or creative writers even to think about the possibility of falling obsessively in love. According to anthropologists, obsessive love is unkown in agrarian societies where people have to work hard just to survive. So in a sense obsessive love can be considered an indulgence, a frippery, something unnecesary to survival.

In fact, throughout history obsessive love has been more or less confined to those who have the leisure for it. In the Middle Ages, the troubadours, the young men who sang passionate love songs to the lady of the castle, were upper-class males who did not have a job or position in society. They had to do something with their time and their emotions, so they wrote or sang love songs to married ladies who were eternally unavailable. The very unavailability allowed the love to appear 'purer' and also gave scope for enormous inventiveness. If the lady did respond, by chance, the young man might have discovered she did not have quite so many charms and perfections as he fondly imagined. There might also have to be some genuine interaction – which might quickly pour cold water on the idealization of the feelings. In some cases the young troubadours probably did not fall deeply in love but just persuaded themselves that they had done so, so as to fend off boredom.

In later times, in the sixteenth and seventeenth centuries, most love poetry was written by young men who had plenty of money and leisure at their disposal and who did not have to work for a living. Sixteenth-century poetry is full of sighings, murmurings, agony, sadness, lack of reciprocity, lack of understanding and complaints about the 'cruelty' of the beloved. All the hallmarks of obsessive love are there.

In Victorian times, the main sufferers from obsessive love were young upper-class women who again had hardly anything to do but wait for marriage. By this time, though, most young men of the upper class were no longer leading lives of such complete leisure, but were sent away to harsh boarding schools and thence to the army or to help govern the Empire while barely out of their teens. They no longer had the time to write impassioned poetry to Stella, Phyllis, Anthea or Laura – who were, in any case, mainly products of the poets' fervid, fevered imaginations rather than being real flesh and blood people.

Upper-class Victorian women were, on the whole, not allowed to be educated properly, and basically had nothing to do but to wait for love to happen. In the meantime they could dream about it, and absorb their time by falling hopelessly in love with any young man who happened to be around. Their dreaming about love might possibly also have been heightened by wearing tight stays, enforced inactivity, lack of exercise and the deliberate cultivation of fragility and illness.

Education

The impact of education is extremely important. The case histories have something else in common – all the besotted lovers are educated people, or people in the process of becoming educated, people who wanted to be educated.

An education which enables people to think about and analyse their feelings, and to read about people who have themselves fallen hopelessly in love, also encourages these feelings to develop. And as already noted, an enormous amount of great literature is about aspects of falling in love. If we read about something enough it is likely that we will be attracted to it – especially as those who have grand passions in their lives always seem more interesting than sober, settled individuals.

Although I said earlier that Victorian upper-class girls fell hopelessly in love partly because they were denied a proper education, they would have been taught 'accomplishments' by a governess. The at-home education they received would have enabled them to reflect on love, and they would have been avid readers of romantic novels, in which heroines fell dramatically and wonderfully in love with tall, dark, handsome heroes.

Feeling vulnerable and not belonging

Although I have put this factor third in the list, it is possibly the most important – the absolute, over-riding one. It helps to explain, at least to some extent, why obsessions appear to happen 'out of the blue', and why you can fall so cataclysmically in love with somebody whom you hardly know.

The whole thing is, of course, extremely complicated. But looking at our analysis so far, who is it that falls obsessively in love? On the whole, people who have leisure, who have had a certain amount of education, but who do not have a recognized place in the world: those who, while intelligent, are not doing a useful job or one which makes them feel fulfilled. Pupils, patients, students – all these are people whose lives are in limbo, have not really begun, or are at a standstill for some reason.

I believe that obsessive love happens only, and solely, at times when there is a great sense of not fitting into your circumstances, of being out on a limb. It is also a danger when you do not feel useful, or sense that you are not performing a useful and important task in the world.

Charlotte Brontë fell in love when alone in Brussels, in a strange country and speaking a strange language. She had no family or friends near her – no circle of acquaintances, even. Moreover, she did not know what she wanted to do with her life. She had the prospect of the school that was planned at the Haworth parsonage, but that did not really excite her; and as yet the possibility of becoming a published writer was as yet a remote and possibly unattainable dream. Elizabeth Smart and Kathleen Raine fell hopelessly in love at periods in their lives when they did not seem to fit into their surroundings; there was not really a 'place' for them. Or they had not found it.

In my own case, I had come to university as the first member of my family to do so, and had arrived in a city where I knew nobody at all. I was reading a subject I didn't like, and had not so far found a congenial circle of friends.

But why should feelings of vulnerability and a sense of not belonging predispose you to such an agonizing experience as obsessive love, which only serves to make everything worse? It really all comes down to that 'urge to merge', to recreate that infantile dependence we once had as small children. In psychological terms, obsessive love constitutes a complete collapse of ego boundaries. You are most likely to experience this collapse when you do not really know who you are, what you want, what you will get, or how to fit into your present circumstances.

In a sense, falling obsessively in love is an attempt to belong, or to feel you belong, by merging yourself so completely with the other person that you feel you are part of this person – not separate at all. Obsessive love is so impervious to reason and rationality precisely because our great longing to merge and belong dates back to the time when we really were dependent, before we had language, and before we really were separate people.

The trouble is, most objects of obsessive love are not 'Mum', but are themselves precarious individuals struggling for recognition and stability. But they *appear* to belong more, and to be more in charge of themselves than the obsessed lover.

When we are babies we do not distinguish between ourselves and the rest of the world. There are no boundaries or separations, and no question of a separate identity. As a child grows up it begins to experience itself as separate from the rest of the world, and gains a sense of 'me'. Ego boundaries – just a technical term for the sense of separateness – gradually develop as the child grows up. But these boundaries can also bring loneliness and a sense of isolation. Accordingly falling in love, or even a crush or unsuitable infatuation, is an attempt at precarious moments to recreate that early sense of belonging, of lack of separation.

It is no accident that crushes commonly happen to teenagers, whose bodies are rapidly changing, whose moods may fluctuate wildly, and who are neither the child they once were nor the adult they will become. And one reason why girls develop crushes more readily than boys may be that girls' bodies undergo more startling and dramatic changes. Boys get tall and develop deep voices and facial hair, but these developments rarely cause problems. With girls, burgeoning breasts and menstruation may bring about a great sense of shame, together with sadness for the loss of childhood innocence and a straight, athletic, boyish body.

And as our society glorifies heterosexual love, the nearest a girl can get to 'merging' is to fall hopelessly in love – always with somebody who seems more confident, more secure, more in charge. One reason why such love causes enormous agony is that the longed-for merging simply does not happen – the object of the affections seems indifferent, or interested only in sex, and there is never the feeling of togetherness which, the besotted one imagines, would make everything all right again.

The American psychiatrist M. Scott Peck says in his bestselling book *The Road Less Travelled* that falling in love can be seen as an act of regression, a return to a childish state. But, he says, falling in love is not an act of will, not something we make a conscious choice to do. However much we may want to fall in love, the experience may still elude us. And in any case, we are as likely to fall in love with somebody unsuitable as with somebody with whom we will be well matched. Falling in love is effortless – it just happens. The more obsessive the love, the more completely the ego boundaries become shattered and the sense of self disappears. No wonder agony results.

For M. Scott Peck, romantic love is a terrible lie – a con-trick of nature to ensure survival of the species by trapping us (frequently) into marriage or other long-term relationship for long enough to reproduce. Obsessive love too may sometimes end in marriage, when the 'beloved' succumbs out of pity or sympathy, as occasionally happens. Such liaisons, though, are almost always a disaster: whenever people fall hopelessly in love, sooner or later they fall out of it – and there may not be much else left to keep the relationship going.

Fear and lack of self-confidence are always heightened at times of dramatic life changes. This is why obsessions so often happen when people leave home for the first time, start a new job or try to establish a new life in another town or country.

Having an inflated opinion of oneself

This is also a very important ingredient of obsessive love. Although at first this factor may appear to contradict the previous one – feelings of vulnerability – in fact having an inflated opinion of oneself always goes with a lack of self-confidence and genuine self-esteem. Somebody who is extremely sure and self-confident, who does not have a strong need to impress and achieve, will probably not fall in love in this way.

On the whole, people do not fall obsessively in love with absolute nobodies. Those who attract in this way always have something about them that you want for yourself – but are not sure that you deserve, or should have. Obsessive love hurts because the ego is offended. If you have an inflated opinion of yourself, you will expect to be loved by somebody who is worthy of you, not just by somebody ordinary. And then, when the love is not returned, you become mortally offended and your ego is bruised and battered.

The agony comes when self-love and ego are too high for genuine love to take place. One very strong characteristic of obsessive love is that sufferers are only ever concerned with themselves – never with the feelings and reactions of the beloved. Much love poetry demonstrates this clearly. And all those who have ever written about obsessive love – including myself in my teenage diaries – are only ever concerned with their own feelings. They never stop to consider what effect they may be having on the other person.

The misery and desolation arise because this inflated opinion has taken a severe knocking, and has put the lover into a precarious and tortured position. Obsession prevents reason, and the obsessed one can never think clearly while the emotions are at their height.

If the love was real, instead of arising from ego, then there would be concern for the other person's wishes and well-being. But as it is, there is only self-pity. It is because the ego is mightily offended by the lack of reciprocity, and because obsession dulls the faculty of reasoning, that obsessed lovers can sometimes inflict terrible suffering on the other person, submitting them to all kinds of unwelcome intrusions and then being mortally wounded when they don't respond. It is because the ego has been hurt, and we have become quite incapable of any empathy with the beloved, that we can ring them twenty times a day, plague them with endless letters, haunt and stalk them. We have lost control over our behaviour.

Falling obsessively in love puts us in a weakened position, in which our equilibrium is severely shaken. Because of inflated self-love and ego, obsessive love can turn to hate and rage.

53

Having particular childhood experiences

Some psychologists who have studied obsessive love believe that an unhappy or dysfunctional childhood is to blame for the phenomenon, and that obsessive love is yet another manifestation of the 'women who love too much' syndrome, in which women torture themselves by falling for men who seem exciting but are actually bad for them. Men can also sabotage themselves by falling in love with unsuitable women, of course.

But it seems to me that the picture is far more complicated than at first appears, and although childhood influences undoubtedly play a part – possibly a very strong one – no clear pattern emerges. There is no standard background that predisposes people to have obsessive affairs, although there may well be clues which can help us to define the syndrome further.

The whole subject of childhood influences being responsible for adult dysfunction is extremely fashionable at the moment, and certainly some types of aberrant adult behaviour do seem to have their origins in a specific type of family background. For instance, it is now known that alcoholics and drug addicts almost always come from backgrounds where there was a great deal of pretence, and where the children were there for the parents, rather than the parents being there for the children. But there is not such a clear-cut and satisfying explanation of why some people succumb to obsessive love.

Obsession sometimes results when there has been a shadowy father-figure, or prolonged absence or death of one parent. For susceptible people, therefore, there may not be the support needed for proper ego development and gaining of a genuine sense of self-identity. This means they become susceptible to having their already fragile ego boundaries shaken whenever the world looks threatening and uncomfortable.

Obsession can also arise when you are the only person in your background to have had a higher education, and there is no background, no knowing how to behave. People who have lived intensely in their imaginations from childhood onwards often form a picture of their ideal man or woman, and then

imagine they have met this person when they encounter somebody who reminds them, in however, watered-down a version,
of this ideal.

Psychotherapist Vera Diamond, who works mainly with
adults traumatized by severe abuse as children, believes that
if we have been badly hurt in early life we may unconsciously
look for somebody who is going to hurt us again. Vera said:
'We always unconsciously look for patterns to repeat, so that
children who have been sexually abused themselves will seek
out abusers in later life. All prostitutes, without exception,
have been abused as children, and they don't consider they
are worth a proper relationship where they are valued for
anything but sex.'

In the same way, those who fall prey to obsessive love
may well have deep feelings of unworthiness, so that although
on the surface they may seem to have a good opinion of
themselves, deep down they may feel unworthy of being
properly loved – so they fall in love with somebody who
doesn't love them back, and punish themselves that way. It
is all unconscious, of course – not carefully thought out
beforehand.

Always feeling special and different

Very many people who fall obsessively in love have always
felt slightly apart, slightly more special, than other people.
This may be because of a certain type of childhood, or they
may possess greater talent and ability than average.

A feeling of being special and different sets you apart from
other people, but not in a way that is comfortable or healthy.
There is little sense of connectedness with others – and, of
course, obsessive love is the very opposite of connectedness.
This sense of being special and different is not an absolute
blueprint for obsessive love, but it renders the possibility far
more likely.

In our present society, starting in the 1940s and 1950s
large numbers of bright children from uneducated working-
class homes went to grammar school and then university and
subsequently entered the professions. Such a thing had never
happened before. They had a 'special and different' feeling –
of wearing a posh uniform and travelling on a bus to school, of

learning Latin and later getting A-levels and leaving home –
but also a great sense of aloneness.

When you are the only bright child in your family, and have
far greater gifts than those around you it is very difficult to
know where you fit in. Obviously your education and attain-
ments set you apart from your family of origin; but you do
not belong to the 'educated' classes either, because you have
no background of culture or learning.

It is perhaps significant that, while I fell hopelessly in love in
my first term at university, my flatmate Penny, who did come
from an educated upper-middle class background, did not –
although she, as much as I, wanted to find that 'special' person
in her life. But Penny had no sense of not belonging – many
members of her family had experienced higher education.

Vera Diamond believes that, in addition to certain childhood
influences and types of background, there is a distinct personality type particularly prone to fall obsessively in love. These
are people who want and seem to need high drama in their
lives. The easy path, the reciprocated, low-key love affair, is not
for them. Everything has to be heightened, intense – possibly
because these people are more imaginative than average. Or,
possibly, more disturbed.

This seems so with most cases of obsessive love. As well
as having inflated self-love and ego, obsessive lovers want to
lead lives that are more exciting, possibly more dangerous,
than usual. If there was no danger, no excitement in your
childhood, you may well manufacture it later.

Consider for a minute the hothouse childhood of Charlotte Brontë. She and her brother and two sisters lived in
an intense world of the imagination, where they invented
impossibly romantic characters who had high-drama adventures and devastating love affairs. So reluctant were they to
leave this world as they grew up that they continued the
fantasies of Gondal and Angria well into adulthood. Indeed,
Emily Brontë never left it – and she never fell obsessively in
love.

But Charlotte, who very much did want to live in the 'real'
world, wanted to meet somebody who was flesh and blood
and was not content to live purely in the imagination. But
with her long background of making up adventures for highly

romantic characters, and with her real-life experiences of having to entertain her father's boring curates and parishioners, it was hardly surprising that she fell headlong in love with the first charismatic man she met.

Most of us who succumb to obsessive love have formed an almost complete picture of what the lover is to look like and how he or she will behave. The longing to have a real-life experience is so great that we imagine ourselves deeply in love with the first person who seems to come anywhere near this idea. As Vera Diamond said, the fact that this person very probably has feet of clay up to the armpits is beside the point – initially, although the penny eventually drops if any kind of reciprocal relationship develops.

One reason that reciprocal relationships often don't develop, though, is because subconsciously we know that if we did get to know this person well they might not be all we imagined. So we conveniently fall in love with somebody who seems unattainable, so that we never will have to face the truth about them.

The aspect of inequality

Whenever obsessive love arises, there is some significant aspect of inequality. The beloved may be married, older, famous, unattainable – or in the case of many male obsessive lovers, too young or too far down the social scale.

In some important way the score is never evened up: imbalance remains. And nothing ever *will* even up the score. Many men fall obsessively in love with very beautiful women, women whom they don't think they can attract in real life. So they content themselves with an obsession. Upper-class men may fall in love with a young girl who seems natural and earthy, unlike the artificial people they meet in their circle. Young girls frequently fall in love with very handsome, striking men – again, men they don't feel really worthy of attracting. So again, obsession develops.

It seems also that those people who bring out obsessive feelings in others are often actually more striking, more noticeable, than ordinary. They also often seem far out of reach, so that instead of having a proper relationship you can only look and long, and put the beloved on a pedestal.

If you have ever fallen victim to obsessive love, look through these seven factors and see which ones apply. And if you know somebody who is desperately in love, or you have been on the recieving end, read them again to see whether any bells ring. You'll probably find they do – loudly.

Is it always an opposite-sex relationship?

So far, we have spoken only of heterosexual obsessive love. So is this a factor, too?

It seems most likely that obsessive love is an extreme version of how society sees love between the sexes. Traditionally, women have fallen in love with and married older, richer, more powerful men, people who have more clout in society than they have themselves, while men have gone for weaker, younger, less well-educated, more passive females. This pattern has been so standard for hundreds of years that it is thought of as completely normal. In fact, women who marry much younger, much less powerful men, and men who go for older, powerful women, are still rare enough to cause comment.

The relatively recent 'toyboy' phenomenon is an illustration of how falling in love and establishing relationships is deeply embedded in our culture, rather than being something entirely normal and natural. Now that women are at last able to gain power, education and income in their own right, they are attracting, and are attracted to, younger men. There is no longer the same overwhelming need for women to fall in love with an older man who will be a proper provider.

Most great literature, and also most pulp fiction, celebrates opposite-sex love. So it is hardly surprising that we enact cultural patterns when we come to fall in love ourselves. We build up expectations, and then try to fulfil them.

In a different kind of culture, same-sex love affairs could follow an identical pattern. It is extremely common for girls in all-girl schools and for boys in all-boy schools to have crushes on teachers or older pupils of the same sex. But officially this is not allowed in our culture; it is seen as an aberration – so most of us oblige by falling in love with somebody of the opposite sex.

There is possibly also, as M. Scott Peck says, a biological imperative, but that is not the whole of the story. In a society where homosexuality was seen as normal, rather than 'queer', I'm sure we would find many more same-sex obsessions. This happened in the First World War, when young men were suffering so terribly in the trenches. Many became obsessed with those in command, who seemed more self-confident and more in control of a horrendous situation. This of course, harks back to another important aspect of obsessive love – we tend to fall in love, in weakened moments, with those who seem to be able to help us to survive.

Is it all illusion?

Sadly, yes. The whole point about obsessive love is that it is illusion, self-generated, something which comes entirely from ourselves and not from the other person. At most, there may be 10 per cent of input from the beloved.

It is all mainly wishful thinking. If you long and long to meet a handsome prince, then sooner or later you will meet one – or at least, somebody who appears to fulfil that function. During obsessive love our senses are blunted and reduced, so that we see the object of our affections wishfully rather than realistically. Whenever you desperately want to experience the feeling of being in love, sooner or later somebody will come along who seems to fulfil all the criteria you have set yourself.

We are so impaired by our own wishfulness that we cannot see what is really there. It's a bit like mothers showing off pictures of their babies. Most mothers truly believe their babies are beautiful, and will rarely be persuaded of the objective truth. To a besotted mother, her baby *is* beautiful. And to an obsessed lover the beloved is truly special – quite different from the rest of humanity.

The lack of genuine rapport is an important aspect of obsessive love, because it means that the lover is able to foist on to the beloved characteristics that they may well not possess in real life. Very often we never get to know the beloved very well, so we can invest them with all kinds of qualities, good and bad, which suit our purposes.

59

Vera Diamond believes that, deep inside, sufferers know the score. They know that their love will be unrequited, but because of their great need they do not and cannot listen to that inner voice. ' For a split second,' she says,

> *we know that this person is not going to love us back, but the brain almost immediately shuts off this information, and acts as if there will be reciprocity. What happens is that there is strong attachment to the dream, to the ideal.*
>
> *We do get a brief warning, but we ignore it, as the obsession has to be played right to the end. In Greek tragedies, there is always a forewarning of what will happen – in the Oedipus tragedy everything is foretold by the oracle, yet nothing can change the inexorable course of events. Macbeth is told by the witches that he will become king but that his heirs will not inherit, and like characters in Greek tragedies, he tries to subvert the prophecy.*
>
> *Yet nothing can change what has been set in motion, and it is the same with obsessive love. We get warnings, we get clear indications from the other person that they are not interested and will we please leave them alone, but nothing makes any difference. There is a kind of awful inevitability about it.*

And if ever the beloved responds enough to the lover to enter into a long-term relationship, or even marriage, the result is inevitably disastrous. The score is never evened up; we fall out of love and discover that this person, this illusion we have erected in our minds, is actually a fallible, imperfect human being much like anybody else.

The crash when they fall off the pedestal is mighty indeed – and shattering to our own illusions. We then start to blame the other person for not coming up to the imagined ideal, for not being 'the person we married'. I am not talking about reciprocal falling in love, when early heady passion may be replaced in time by a lower-key genuine relationship, but one where there has been great inequality – where one person has fallen headily in love and the other, while feeling basically indifferent, has responded out of pity or sympathy, or out of a wish to settle down.

The question of sex

In the distant past, obsessive affairs were often physically unconsummated. Now, it is highly likely that an obsessive relationship will have some element of sex in it, even where there is no reciprocity, simply because physical sex has become such an everyday occurrence.

But here again illusion prevails. Since the sexual revolution of the sixties we have very much confused love and sex – believing, or wanting to believe, that genital contact and emotional intimacy are much the same thing. But when sex is part of an obsessive relationship this will be just as unsatisfactory as all other aspects of the affair, and may even serve to heighten the emptiness, the lack of genuine rapport, which would characterize a genuine relationship.

We may long and long for physical fusion, but it will never bring about any real closeness. There will always be intense irritation on the part of the 'beloved' that the sex is as bad as everything else about the relationship and does not bring about the hoped-for transcendence.

Nowadays young people of both sexes long for the experience of sex – and this may well be yet another factor in the development of obsessive love. The idea that young women are avid for sexual experience is a new one in our society, dating back only to the fifties and sixties. But now that we have taken it on board, we want it to be wonderful. Young women who fall obsessively in love long above all else to have sex with somebody 'special', somebody 'worthy', not just an ordinary male. Often, when sex has taken place, the obsession becomes even more heightened – and may constitute an even greater trauma than if it doesn't happen. But the relationship will never come right, whatever.

Why doesn't obsessive love ever vanish?

It may seem strange that, far from vanishing as time goes on, the feelings of those who have been obsessively in love but never entered into a proper relationship with the other person get stronger as time goes by. Why doesn't time heal this particular wound?

This aspect will be more fully explored in Chapter 4, but the main reason is because the experience constitutes a major trauma. Whenever a person has been traumatized, the survival instinct comes into play to make them forget and suppress the great hurt that has been done.

People who had been in wartime concentration camps behaved like this. The ones who survived seemed to forget all about the experience and to cope wonderfully well. In some cases it even seemed that it had not been such a great trauma, after all. But in later life, as they got older and perhaps more physically frail, the experience came back to haunt them. It became so nightmarish that sometimes they committed suicide. Two famous concentration camp victims, the writer Primo Levi and the influential American psychologist and author Bruno Bettelheim, eventually killed themselves after leading extremely successful lives after their release. It caught up with them – and they could not bear it.

We tend to keep traumatic experiences firmly locked behind the steel doors of the mind and emotions. What we often don't appreciate is that a lot of energy is taken up with keeping this secret under wraps so that it will never return to haunt us, and it can never be spoken about to anybody else. But in time the knocking at the steel door get louder and louder, and eventually the experience tends to break through and be remembered. It often happens when we simply haven't got the energy to contain it any more, or when we are weakened or elderly or ill.

The only real way to rid ourselves of traumatic experiences in the past, whether these are of child abuse, the trauma that follows bereavement or other severe loss, or obsessive love, is to relive them so that they can be released. This is what I did, eventually, with dramatically beneficial results. Once it has held us in its thrall, obsessive love never goes away of its own accord, however much we might want it to. It has to be helped away. The great lovers of the past saw their affairs end tragically. Nowadays, thanks to new therapies, new understanding, we can heal the wound caused by this cataclysmic emotion and emerge as whole, loving people once more. Once we can discharge the negative residual emotions we can even feel benevolent towards the person who has obsessed us and who, we may imagine, has hurt us so badly in the past.

Part Two

RECOVERY

4 Facing Up to Yourself

It's never easy to take a decision to undergo therapy to try and uncover traumatic incidents from the past. For one thing, there is no knowing just how painful the whole thing is going to be; and for another, at the back of one's mind there is always the question: can I trust the therapist? Will he or she help me to put myself together – or make me disintegrate even more? And will I be able to handle what might come up, when memories are hazy and the incident is, consciously at least, half-forgotten, buried? It was with these misgivings in mind that I paid my second visit to Morning Light to undergo the therapy which would, it was hoped, enable me to relive and release my own trauma of obsessive love, and to emerge stronger for letting it out of the system.

The owners of Morning Light, a modest guest house four-teen miles outside Pitlochry in Scotland, had written to me in connection with an article on therapy I had written in a Sunday newspaper. I liked the tone of their letter, and had already been impressed with the work they were doing with adult victims of child abuse. I felt that their methods were sensible, healing, and could very probably help me. I had a feeling that the time was right to deal with the situation, as my apparently chance meeting with my former boyfriend had left me feeling extremely disturbed.

Many psychologists now say that whenever an incident triggers off a wholly inappropriate reaction, as the stomach-churning when talking to my former boyfriend seemed to be, then we should take notice and try to get to the bottom of it. Whenever something which should not make us personally angry does, or whenever an ordinary event makes us feel uncomfortable or disturbed, it is likely that something deeper, something which we have tried to bury, is bothering us — and trying to get out into the open.

Through years of practice the therapists at Morning Light have evolved their own methods, which do not easily fit into any psychoanalytic school but which have been shown to work. After my initial visit there I was convinced not only that they were completely genuine, but that they actually did help people — more than can be said for all analysis or therapy.

The sessions themselves consist of the subject lying on a bed or couch while the therapist encourages a journey back in time to when the trauma began, or to when it started to affect the individual. Questions are asked, always in the present tense, so that if the subject is attempting to recall something that happened at the age of five the therapist will treat him or her as a child of five, expecting the reactions of a child of that age. By this method long-hidden traumas can often begin to come out, although it is frequently a stop-start process as there can be strong resistance and denial.

The idea is to discharge the hurt, so that life is no longer lived under its burden. Another aim is to stop blaming oneself, or others, for what cannot be changed — and to go foward into the future with a new and more positive attitude and energy.

Sessions are not timed, and each person is given as long as they seem to need — it is not unusual for a session to last several hours. Everything is taped: an important part of the therapy is the 'listening back' with somebody sympathetic and non-judgemental. People are encouraged to 'listen back' at the earliest opportunity and are often surprised at what they hear, since during therapy subjects often go into an altered state of consciousness — even though they are not hypnotized as such.

The two therapists, Veronica Stephenson and Clive Malcouronne, who have been working in this way for more than fifteen years, do not charge for the actual therapy — only for bed and board. The centre is residential, as Clive and Veronica feel that the good achieved in therapy can often be almost immediately undone when people have to return to their ordinary lives and jobs while still in a raw, vulnerable state.

During my own therapy sessions I was amazed at how much I remembered, and also how emotional I was at times during the questioning. Having always considered myself a cool and rational person, I was at times surprised by the emotional nature of my reactions.

The therapy

Before therapy proper proceeds, Veronica or Clive ask pertinent questions, so that with any luck, the nitty-gritty can be accessed immediately without wasting time talking about inessentials. Then Veronica took me back to the age of four, and started asking me questions about my childhood. I was not hypnotized, was perfectly aware of what I was saying – and felt perfectly secure to talk about things I had never mentioned to anybody before.

It emerged that my childhood had been a relatively happy one, although my father was alcoholic and I did not have a good relationship with him. But until the age of ten or so I was brought up mainly by my grandparents and a maiden aunt. The most overwhelming thing to emerge from my childhood was this feeling of being special and different, mentioned in Chapter 3 as one of the possible factors predisposing to obsessive love. There had also been a strong feeling of not belonging to my family of origin, of being a 'little princess' living among peasants. I was the first member of my family to go to university.

That first session, which lasted about three months, ended with me at the age of eighteen and about to go to university, feeling very confident and successful as I had done well in my A-levels, and considering myself quite smart and sophisticated, bohemian and anarchic. I had been a stalwart ban-the-bomber, going on several marches, and was interested in art and literature. I had a horror of being 'bourgeois' in those days; I certainly wanted to make some kind of impact, though quite what I had no idea. But I certainly had a high opinion of myself, coupled with feelings of vulnerability and not belonging. After all, I was venturing into a world completely unknown – that of higher education and living hundreds of miles from home.

The incident was relived during the second therapy session, which took place the following day. What astonished me more than anything else was how raw, how unhealed by time were my feelings concerning John. We went through seeing him in a queue, trying to meet him, coming up against the wall of his indifference and inviting him to all those parties, stalking, haunting and dreaming about him. All the time Veronica asked questions about my feelings, trying to get me to describe how I felt at each stage, what emotions I was going through.

I was asked to describe John physically, and although I had not seen him since 1965 and had no pictures of him I seemed to remember every detail, down to the exact colour of his eyes. I could do this even though I had consciously tried to suppress all memories of him. Veronica asked me what was so special about him, and intimated that I was clearly feeling some kind of effect from him – that here, to me, was somebody who stood out from the crowd. The 'specialness' I felt he had was overwhelming attractiveness – he seemed to be not just handsome, but intriguing, different, set apart somehow. He also had an air of confidence which was extremely noticeable.

'When you're talking to him, do you feel you're talking to somebody you've known for ever?' Veronica asked.

I replied that he didn't seem to be a stranger, even though I had never met him before. Nobody had ever had this effect on me previously, I added and I was powerless to control or even understand it. But, like the French Lieutenant's Woman in the novel by John Fowles, once I saw him I was lost.

And it was horribly uncomfortable. The feelings of great fear, lack of confidence, not knowing how to behave, not being in control and being taken over all tumbled out. There was a great deal of shame attached to these emotions, and a very strong feeling of guilt, that I was to blame. Veronica said she thought the experience was ego-shattering for me, as I seemed to be losing all sense of identity. She suggested that John was playing cat and mouse with me – not being interested or not showing interest, and yet giving the impression that he found me attractive when at parties or other gatherings. At the same time I recalled his intense irritation with the way I followed him around.

I had a certain amount of amnesia about the actual experience of sex — something which still can't be recalled in any great detail, except that penetration was achieved only with enormous difficulty. I recalled that he seemed extremely blasé about the whole thing, as if he seduced teenagers every day of the week, but mentioned that it was also a big effort and difficult for him. He was, I recalled, much more sexually experienced than me.

It emerged that my feelings for John had been overwhelmingly passionate, that I was in no doubt that I loved him so much, but was also aware that he didn't care at all about me. I mentioned knowing somehow that we would never have a proper relationship — it had made me feel very upset, but anything was better than nothing.

After the experience had been relived it was time for analysis. Veronica suggested: 'You know, there's a song, "Falling in love with love is falling for make-believe." And sometimes we have this inner awareness of the ideal, and you feel you've recognised it, and something within John triggered off a recognition. But later on, you find it's a reflection of the ideal rather than the real ideal.'

She added that it is often easy to confuse a reflection of an ideal with the reality, and I replied that John very probably did represent some externalization of an ideal I had formulated in my own mind. Veronica felt that I was probably a conquest for him, and that having achieved it there was no longer any mileage for him in pursuing the relationship.

She went on to ask what personal needs I imagined John fulfilled. Certainly the physical, I said (I was determined to experience sex as soon as possible after getting to university — it was just a question of finding the right person), but I added that I had been nervous and frightened of actually doing it. He also seemed to fulfil intellectual needs. I felt that he was intellectual and literary rather than being 'macho', and was sensitive and poetic even if not possessing any great literary gifts. He certainly took a very active part in the arts life of the university, producing magazines and plays. He seemed to have the confidence to do so.

Also, what was possibly even more important was that, unlike most other first year students, he hadn't come straight from school. He had been out in the world and had travelled – all of which was at the time quite outside my experience; and because of this he seemed glamorous, remote and superior.

So what need didn't he fulfil, Veronica asked.

Clearly he didn't fulfil an emotional need because I never had a proper relationship with him, and he never showed any genuine interest in me. The effect was shock, illness, trauma.

We then went through the various illnesses that I suffered after he cut off contact with me. I said that my great love then turned to hatred, a bitter hatred which had continued up to the present. During the therapy, all the long bottled-up resentment I had held for John came out. I said that previously I had never known unkindness, had never in my life been treated badly, never been rejected – and so it was all a terrible shock to the ego and resulted in enormous lack of self-respect. During the reliving of this period of my life, I was aware of painful, physical stomach-churning as the events and emotions were recalled.

Then began the healing part of the therapy. Veronica reminded me that, while I had lost my self-respect, my dignity and my identity, I had now regained them all. I had survived; in fact I had probably emerged stronger for the experience than I might otherwise be. Even so, the time had come to release it and untie the knot which bound me to the past. This would enable me finally to let go of the negative feelings I had held for so long – both of blaming myself and of feeling guilty and ashamed of my behaviour – and of my resentment towards John, who in many ways had been the innocent bystander.

'At the time,' she said, 'you were demoralized, devastated. You lost yourself. You became a victim. But now you are a survivor, so you can let go of that pain from the past. It's like distant drums – no longer relevant to your current experience. It's only relevant in so much as it's remaining in your subconscious as a painful experience you haven't let yourself get over.'

The effect of the therapy

After two three-hour sessions, this aspect of the therapy was over. The effect was strange. The first thing I noticed was that I did start to feel differently about John. Instead of the memory being something murky in my background and hedged around with negative emotions concerning him, I was now able to see him more clearly as he was – a young, insecure man, and not the embodiment of Lucifer or Dracula.

This effect was heightened during the 'listening back' sessions, where it became clear to me for the first time that John was actually doing his best to let me know he wasn't interested and was trying to be nice about it. But at the same time he remained intrigued enough to want to have sex. After 'listening back', I found I was able to forgive John and forgive myself. Obviously it had not particularly hurt him that I had carried around his huge burden of resentment for more than a quarter of a century, but it had not done me very much good. I realized that it had meant that during my adult life I had never been able to respond fully to people, that a large part of my energies was taken up with containing this hurt from the past.

Also, I had 'chloroformed' myself by immersing myself in my career, family and homemaking – all enjoyable and valid activities – but they had served as a kind of anaesthetic over the years. I made myself too busy for much introspection. It was only when the anaesthetic was wearing off, when the family had grown up, when my marriage had ended and when my career was relatively firmly established, that the emotions started knocking on the door again, begging to be let out.

I had always known that there was a block of frozen emotions which I could not access or remove in any way, but had no idea until the therapy that it was due to this affair. I would not have believed that an affair which was so brief, so unsatisfactory, so one-sided, could possibly have left such a lasting hurt. But the passions and strong emotions which came out in therapy could not be denied.

People often wonder how much that is apparently recalled during therapy is 'fantasy' and how much is real. They are also afraid that, if they go into an altered state of consciousness or undergo actual hypnosis, the therapist might be putting ideas into their head.

I cannot speak for anybody else, but what I can say from direct experience is that it actually seemed impossible to lie, impossible to fantasize, impossible to tell anything except the truth. I could not remember in every detail what had happened, and I'm sure some of the incidents were slightly different from my recollection, but what came out more strongly than anything else was my emotional reaction to these events.

Once or twice during therapy I dimly thought: I'm not putting myself in a very good light. What can I do to seem less wimpish, more like a woman of the world? Yet I could not help what I had said.

People have since asked me if there was anything which happened during therapy which could not have come out simply from talking to a friend. The answer is that there is very little similarity to talking to a friend. Apart from the fact that friends would probably not be very interested in a six-hour sob story of a long-ago affair, they would be unlikely to understand how great was the trauma and upset that the incident left.

I certainly came away from Morning Light feeling a very different person. It was as if all my adult life I had been carrying round a heavy rucksack full of rubbish − without even realizing I was carrying it. The strongest effect was that an enormous amount of pent-up energy was released. This initially took the form of disturbing sexual feelings − not for anybody in particular, but just feelings which rose up of their own accord. I mentioned this to Veronica, who said that from her experience after therapy all the emotions are shaken up and may take some time to settle down.

Meeting John again

Helpful as the therapy had been, I did not feel it quite completed the story. There was a strong feeling of unfinished business − that I could not finally close the chapter until I had met John again. Veronica Stephenson thought it might be a good idea to try and meet him, but the question was: how? I had not seen him for twenty-five years, and had no idea, even, whether he was alive or dead.

In the event it took me about half an hour to track him down. A mutual friend told me that John had been divorced for many years, but that his ex-wife still lived in the same part of the country. I got her number from directory enquiries, and rang it. She told me that John now lived in Singapore and was about to move to Australia, but that he was in the UK for a few weeks, staying with his grown-up daughter, to finish his PhD. She gave me the number in Wales, not asking why I wanted to contact him.

With heart pounding, I rang the number. A deep, unfamiliar, gruff voice eventually answered. When I told him who I was, and reminded him that we had been at university together, he said, still gruffly: 'Whatever made you drag up my name after all these years?'

I told him that it didn't have to be dragged far, that I was working on a book about young love (I felt that 'obsessive love' at this stage might be too strong), but added that I had never been able to forget him. I wondered if he might be able to meet me to discuss what had happened all those years ago.

He had difficulty recalling me. 'Were you one of my students?' he asked.

No, I said, I was a contemporary of his.

He thought again. 'Do you have very black hair and blue eyes?'

'No,' I said. 'I do have black hair, but I've never had blue eyes.' We talked for another ten minutes or so – about the subject matter of his PhD, about his life in the intervening years – and I could see that he was desperately trying to get some picture of me. But nothing much came.

In the morning, however, he rang back – recollections having returned in glorious technicolor, and not without a certain amount of pain either. He now remembered exactly who I was and said that he had a very clear picture of me. This time he sounded quite different and much more friendly, although he remained evasive about meeting up.

On the phone, as we talked about our relationship, I told

him I had been desperately in love with him, and that the emotions aroused had resulted in my going completely out of control. I had remembered John as a rather arrogant young man – but he seemed to have changed. He was extremely sympathetic, told me that he himself had been in counselling for very many years, and that he completely understood the need to 'lay the ghost' and unpack the debris from the past so that it could no longer exert its influence on the present. He asked if we had ever gone out together, and I told him, well, not exactly, but we had had a sexual relationship. He immediately remembered the occasion, and said it had been horribly painful and traumatic for him.

He was, he told me, trying hard to finish his PhD – after twenty-three years! – and had developed a mysterious foot problem which caused his ankles to swell and immobilized him. He had seen doctors, but nobody had been able to explain what it was. John's own explanation was that it was subconsciously self-induced so that he would not be able to move until the thesis was finished. He said that he could not walk far, and had not been out of the house for three or four weeks.

I sensed a reluctance to meet, although we exchanged several long and valuable telephone calls – the first proper conversations I had ever had with him. Eventually he rang and said he didn't think we would be able to meet as he couldn't get his PhD finished, and had to be back in Singapore on a certain date.

I said that if the worst came to the worst we could always meet at the airport – which is what eventually happened. I was determined that one way or another I could not let him go back to the Far East without at least seeing him and replacing the 1963 tape that was running in my head with a more current one. Perhaps he really was worried about the PhD, or perhaps he was reluctant for other reasons to meet me; but anyway, he agreed to meet me at the check-in desk for his flight.

During the weeks when I was speaking to him, I was in a state of heightened emotion and trepidation. All my nerve endings were on edge again, and on the day I was due to meet him at the airport I felt like a teenager, sick with anticipation.

I was at the check-in desk quite half an hour before we were due to meet – not wanting to miss him under any circumstances. On this mild December day Heathrow was curiously uncrowded. But would I recognize John? He said that without doubt he would recognize me, although I reminded him that I was now middle-aged, not the young person he once knew.

Eventually I saw a man who just had to be John – middle-aged, tall, with grey hair, grey beard, grey tracksuit trousers and carpet slippers on his feet. With him were two much younger people – his daughter and her boyfriend, who had driven him to the airport.

I went up to him, hardly aware of what I was doing. I tried to appear as calm and normal as possible, and in order to gain a level of detachment attempted to view this encounter as a journalistic assignment. I certainly didn't want to appear nervous. 'Are you John?' I asked, as I approached him.

'Yes,' he said and smiled. We shook hands, and then arranged to meet in the restaurant downstairs. I'd done it! I'd met him! After about ten minutes he made his way slowly and painfully to the café, his swollen feet obviously still bothering him.

We had a cup of tea and then talked, talked, talked about the relationship, his attitude towards it, his life, thoughts, aspirations, hopes and ideas. It was all just wonderful, and I was delighted to meet a warm-hearted, open-minded, intelligent and non-egotistical individual whose memory had caused me so much anguish over the years.

As he sat down, he said with a smile: 'It's no big deal, is it? A middle-aged bloke with crippled feet?'

I said: 'That's not really the point – it's what I've had to deal with inside myself that's the problem.'

We spoke honestly about the sexual aspect of the relationship; John blamed himself for the failure of the afternoon to bring us together. He also felt it was a failure because we didn't know each other very well at that point. Gradually, as we talked and he told me about his unusual and adventurous life, I realized that either I had picked up a very wrong impression of him all those years ago or he had changed beyond recognition.

I had certainly considered him a rather ruthless womanizer and, having nothing to erase that impression, that was how

I regarded him still. Whatever he may have been like then, or whatever impression he gave out (and at university there were rumours circulating about him being something of a heart-breaker), nothing could have been further from the truth now.

He asked me what I had expected, and ruefully pointed to his granddad slippers – the only footwear he could manage with his mysterious foot problem. I told him that I had formulated an *Educating Rita* image of a somewhat gnarled academic, as played by Michael Caine in the film. The impression was, as it turned out, fairly accurate. I had picked it up from this voice and conversation on the phone.

In every way he was full of delightful surprises, and I became aware that I was talking to an exceptionally nice man with many unusual qualities – qualities which had led him from being a university lecturer in linguistics, to being a self-employed builder, to erecting his own house from a ruin in Italy, and to living and teaching in Libya and Singapore. He had also, he told me, undergone a kind of nervous breakdown and this had catapulted him into a life quite different from teaching in an English university. He withheld nothing, and was not trying to give either a good or a false impression of himself.

My feelings towards him during this meeting were those of extreme warmth and benevolence. I was glad to realize that the hostility and resentment I had harboured for so many years had quite vanished and that my other fear, that of reactivating the hopeless love I once had for him, was also groundless.

It was a wonderful bonus that he, like me, had worked on himself, having been in counselling for the past eight years, and that he was interested in personal growth. Since his divorce he had not remarried, and seemed happy to be single.

After talking for about an hour and a half it was time for him to go into the departure lounge to board his plane – and this time, instead of a formal handshake we gave each other a huge hug. It seemed entirely natural – and spontaneous.

Then he disappeared out of my life again. It would not be an exaggeration to say that I walked back as if on air, and felt as if I had finally shed the remnants of the emotional burden. After I had been to Morning Light, and after I had met John, a number of people remarked that I looked different, and seemed to be behaving differently — more relaxed, laid-back.

At first I had been afraid of going for therapy, and I had certainly been afraid of contacting and meeting John. Now I know that there was nothing to fear — and that extricating a dark secret from the past, and bringing it out into the open, is always therapeutic. Letting sleeping dogs lie, or imagining that because an incident happened long ago in the past one must have 'got over it by now', are not recipes for emotional health. It certainly can be therapeutic to talk over incidents like this with sympathetic friends, but there is nothing to touch actually reliving and re-experiencing the event. Only then, when the source of the problem has been tapped, can any real healing take place.

It may seem as though there is little that you can do if caught in the grip of obsessive love. But actually there are a number of self-help measures which can ease the burden and lessen the pain. It's all a matter of understanding what is happening. In Chapter 5 we will look at how you can help to free yourself from a hopeless obsession for another person.

5 Self-help Strategies

If you've ever been obsessively in love, the chances are that you made strenuous efforts to keep it all to yourself. Very few people ever admit their feelings in this troubled area, even to themselves. The tendency is to fictionalize, fantasize, minimize and deny – anything but face the truth. This is because it's a trauma, and the unconscious mind always tries to suppress memories and experiences of trauma and prevent them from seeping through to the conscious mind.

Even when the obsession is at its height, the intellectual, analytical and reasoning side of the brain may try to say: this isn't really happening, it's not affecting me at all and I'm not really experiencing it. Therefore there may be protestations of indifference, lack of concern and an attempt at a blasé approach – all to hid the truth, even from yourself.

Severe trauma always brings about a tendency to deny the reality. And obsessive love has much in common with all other shameful secrets from which we try to protect ourselves. People often deny that they are alcoholic or homosexual, have an eating problem, were abused as children or did not have loving parents. We deny because of our shame. And because we deny, society denies.

The word 'denial' has a somewhat technical meaning here – more than simply not admitting that something is the case. It means that we have actually wiped it out of our consciousness, until we no longer even know what is the reality. Psychologists and others treating victims of addiction often speak of them as being 'in denial', which means that they will rationalize their behaviour and blame others for it. For instance, a compulsive eater may say she has big bones, low metabolism, glandular trouble; an alcoholic may sincerely believe he doesn't drink much, or certainly not enough to be labelled alcoholic, and in any case other people make him drink. At its heart, denial is a refusal to face responsibility for our actions. The reason we refuse to face up to the truth is because it is too painful for us.

At the same time as the denial persists, great shame is attached to the behaviour. We know, within ourselves, that something is not right, and this means that we continue to have a low opinion of ourselves. The other danger of denial and shame is that we are not really able to communicate properly with other people. Because we do not know ourselves, or cannot admit the reality of ourselves, we cannot admit other people's reality. This means that we continue to live in a world of illusion and make-believe.

It is not until we are able to face up to the burdens of the past and shed them that we can move on, freed from their influence. 'Personal growth' is a term much in vogue these days, and it really means the ability to know oneself, to empathize with other people and to feel in harmony with one's surroundings and environment. Until 'personal growth' is achieved there is a continual sense of alienation, of being a victim, of not being in control – although paradoxically, all those people who are in denial try rigidly to control both themselves and other people. This is because they are desperately afraid of going out of control, knowing in some part of themselves that they are sitting on a volcano which will, if they are not careful, erupt all around them with devastating consequences.

It is because we deny our shameful secrets that obsessive love has been seen as a 'grand passion', as just a more intense version of falling in love, or being in love. What has really happened is that all control has been lost, that we have become addicted to somebody without understanding why or what it's all about. It's easy to give this kind of obsession the label 'love' – and to attempt to elevate it in this way. Certainly much easier than to admit it's something rather sick. As a society, we are only just learning how liberating and healing it can be to shed secrets from the past, to admit them to ourselves, so that the hurt can be healed and we can live our lives free from the horrible murk of emotions lying just below the surface.

But how can you know for sure whether your love is obsessive – or a wonderful, heady passion? There are several danger signs:

- You fall, or appear to fall, hopelessly in love with somebody you don't even know
- You can't stop thinking or dreaming about this person, even though you may not have exchanged any words
- When you do get to know this person a little, you never seem able to have a proper relationship
- There is a strong sense that your sense of separate identity is being lost
- You find yourself making all sorts of excuses as to why this person never returns your phone calls, goes out with other people, seems not to care about you
- The most overwhelming feeling you have is one of agony, rather than ecstasy or happiness
- Your life is increasingly being narrowed to the point where the only important thing is to be with this person, or to see him/her – not even necessarily to talk or exchange ideas
- You feel unaccountably diminished in the presence of the loved one, as if you don't matter, don't exist
- You experience wild extremes of feeling – surges of love followed by hate
- The beloved seems to hate you and tries to avoid you
- You don't know how to behave. You feel you are breaking the rules, without knowing what the rules are
- You can't seem to eat or sleep properly
- You are losing interest in your appearance
- Your health is suffering
- There is an unaccountable urge to write poetry. (This is all right if you write poetry ordinarily, but not if you've never even considered doing this before)
- There is a terrible feeling of isolation, a feeling that nobody has ever suffered like this before
- You imagine nobody can possibly understand how you feel
- In despair, you have entertained thoughts of suicide or, perhaps, murder – however much in fantasy these remain

- Your beloved is somehow unavailable or unattainable, because of marriage, class, age, sexual orientation or some other apparently insurmountable barrier
- You would love to be able to capture and lock up your beloved, so that you could have this person all to yourself
- You wish you could get over it, and that life would get back to normal
- You feel that all these problems would be solved in an instant if only the beloved would respond.

If all these things characterize obsessive love, what is 'healthy' love, by contrast?

Nobody has ever succeeded in defining it exactly, but whatever true love is, it's certainly worlds apart from obsession. True love encompasses these elements:

Mutuality

There is reciprocity, rapport, a true exchange of ideas, equality.

Respect

You truly love a person when you have enormous respect for them, and want the best for them.

Detachment

True love means the ability to be separated from your nearest and dearest without pining, being in abject misery or experiencing longing feelings. It is being able to let go, to let the other person live his or her own life, to express their individuality. It is wanting the very best for that person − but not being needy yourself.

Fun

True love means you can have fun and laughter together. Obsession makes each of you miserable.

Enjoyment of each other's company

You love to be together, because you have so much in common. Yet you can be happy with or without the company of this person.

Ability to be separate

True, mature love is characterized by re-establishment of ego boundaries. You have a close bond, but have not merged, or attempted to merge, into one another.

There are no guilt feelings

You feel emotionally free, strong, powerful, in control.

If all these feelings are present — congratulations. You are experiencing genuine love, not obsession. Obsession, though, is unfortunately very much more common than true love, and can actually drive love away. That's why it must first be admitted, then faced.

Admitting the obsession

The very first step towards recovery must be the ability to admit the obsession. Obviously it is never easy to admit that you may have gone out of control, that you loved somebody who did not return the feelings, that you were foolish enough to become besotted by somebody who rejected you. All these admissions are painful — it may seem so much more comforting to pretend that it never happened, to suppress the memory, or persuade yourself that the 'beloved' was a cad and a rotter.

As with any other addiction (and obsessive love has much in common with an addiction) it seems much simpler to try and maintain the fiction of being in control, or pretending to oneself that the other person was responsible for what happened. 'He/she made me do it,' is the classic cry of the arch-denier, and an attempt to evade responsibility for one's own actions. Of course rakes, Casanovas, money-grabbers, heartless seducers, sirens, nymphomaniacs and so on do exist, but that is beside the point. If you've fallen for one, then *you* are responsible for what happens as a result.

What you can do

Try to be aware first of all that you are falling in love not with a real person but with an illusion, a fantasy, a projection of all your own hopes, fears and ideals. It has been estimated that in obsessive love about 90 per cent of your feeling is projection – what you have foisted on to the other person coming from your own needs – and only about 10 per cent is real and comes from the other person.

Try to be aware that with obsessive love you are falling mainly for some externalized aspect of yourself, rather than for a real flesh and blood person. With obsession you do not love them for themselves, but for what they represent to you. Realize that falling in love in this way, where there is no mutuality, no rapport, is actually very easy and requires no effort at all. It is self-indulgence – which is why it can never turn into real love.

The reason that obsessions happen so often at vulnerable or difficult times in our lives is precisely because they are so easy – it's like losing yourself rather than gaining yourself, and it takes no hard work to become obsessed. It can, of course, *seem* as though effort is being put into the relationship, simply because all the hours spent sighing, agonizing, writing letters, phoning, stalking and haunting the beloved are so exhausting.

It is vital to understand that the suffering experienced by the lover is not the fault of the beloved. Because obsessive love is self-generated the suffering is self-generated as well. The suffering happens because the ego and *amour propre* are offended – and it is also extremely stressful to experience such strong, conflicting emotions.

I realize from bitter experience that it is not easy to face up to these realities, and that an understanding of what happens may not be enough to cause the passion to disappear. It can be extremely hard to accept that this person whom you seem to love so much, so desperately and absolutely, can be entirely indifferent about you.

When we are obsessed we are in an altered state of consciousness, and may for a time be actually incapable of listening to words of reason – much as an alcoholic cannot get a grip on himself when under the influence: he has to become sober first.

But even if you cannot help obsessive thoughts intruding, these practical Dos and Don'ts will at least help you to cope while the passion is at its most searing.

DON'T send love letters

If you feel a strong urge to send passionate letters to the beloved, bearing in mind that obsessive love can make good — or at least frequent — correspondents of us all, then by all means write them, but DON'T SEND THEM. Instead, a couple of weeks after you have written them look at the letters in a more sober light, and see how they come across to you.

It is very likely that they will seem full of self-pity and self-indulgence, rather than being the fervent, impassioned love poetry you first thought. Keep the letters you write until the obsession no longer seems so dangerous, as they can constitute helpful therapy; but whatever you do, don't send them. Make it a rule that you will send letters only when you are in a calm state of mind, not when you are beside yourself with frenzy and agitation. The recipient may simply not be able to handle such raw emotion.

Golden rule: only ever send passionate love letters when the love is returned, when there is equality, commitment and hope for a future together.

DON'T phone

Again, this is difficult advice to follow, but don't telephone when in an agitated state. It will always have the very opposite effect from the one you intended. Objects of obsessive love are never impressed by intimations of desperate longing — it makes them feel guilty, and this will have the effect of making them reject you even more.

If you feel you can ring your lover up when in a calm condition for a chat, then do so. But never impose any ultimatum, never rant and rave, and never reproach them.

DON'T make pleas

Another golden rule. This person owes you nothing, not even decent behaviour. Because the love is not returned, the beloved has no obligations at all. And impassioned pleas usually result in the beloved shutting off even more.

DON'T blame the beloved

Even in your innermost thoughts never blame the beloved for wrecking your life, for causing you great unhappiness and despair, for putting you through hell. However it seems, you're putting *yourself* through it, and only you can get yourself out of it. Blame is completely irrelevant.

Not blaming does not, of course, mean that the beloved's behaviour is necessarily good or to be condoned; his or her behaviour may well be less than impeccable. For example, very many men on the receiving end of obsessive affection will enter into a sexual relationship with the woman who loves them so obsessively. This leads us on to the next essential Don't.

DON'T have sex

This advice may be particularly hard to follow, as the possibility of sex can make the obsessed one feel that the passion is being returned, that closeness is near. But it never is.

Never embark on a sexual relationship until you can be sure that your affections are genuinely returned. Women especially, when hopelessly in love, can persuade themselves that the man's indifference will be overcome if she gives herself to him through sex. But sex never solves relationship difficulties of this kind – it only ever adds to them, and increases the sum of misery. Sex never of itself makes the heart grow fonder – it makes it grow colder, because the disappointment that follows it, when no real intimacy results, is so bitter.

We confuse love and sex, often imagining them to be part and parcel of the same thing. But when there is one-sided obsession, sex will be as bad as everything else about the relationship.

And don't make the mistake of becoming promiscuous as a way of drowning your sorrows. This is simply employing one drug to try and deaden the effect of another.

DON'T fantasize

A very difficult piece of advice to follow. It is tempting to imagine that if only the feelings were returned, if only you were going out together, if only you were married, then everything would be wonderful. The likelihood is that any permanent relationship would be even worse, if anything, than the obsessional fantasies. Neediness of any kind is not a good basis for a permanent relationship.

And now some important Dos.

DO keep busy

Obsessive love thrives above all on idleness. So an excellent form of self-therapy is to keep as busy as possible with non-intellectual but manually demanding tasks such as breadmaking, gardening, do-it-yourself, dressmaking – anything which is absorbing but has an enjoyable end result. Hard physical work which results in pleasant fatigue is a marvellous antidote to obsessive feelings about another person.

All this activity won't necessarily make the feelings go away completely, but you will be given a valuable respite from the mental agony and stress. The less physical work you have to do, the more likely obsessive feelings are to grow.

In addition, the busier and more active you are the easier you will find it to sleep at night, which will give you strength to face the following day. Of course you will still be preoccupied with the beloved, but when such thoughts arise go with them and try to sort them out. Never try to pretend they are not there, or believe they will go away of their own accord. Obsessive thoughts must be dealt with in one of two ways: either replace them with healthier thoughts, or work through them by facing them and trying to deal with them.

DO think positively about yourself

In many ways, it is low self-esteem which has precipitated this feeling, and your confidence is likely to be at a pretty low ebb during and after an obsession. It is important that you put this restless energy to some useful purpose, rather than allowing it to dwell on the object of your obsessive love.

Self-confidence can be built up through learning a new skill, such as playing the piano or learning a language, or going to aerobics or yoga classes – anything which produces quick or noticeable results. When you *see* results, you will have a better view of yourself. Using affirmations – repeating positive statements about yourself – will also help to make you feel better and stronger inside.

DO keep a diary

This can be most valuable. Note down exactly how you feel and what is happening. Many people keep diaries and journals in times of anguish: the trouble is that when reading them back it may seem as if the whole of that period was one of unbearable agony. In fact, this will not be the case.

When keeping a diary, record not only the anguish but also the happy things you did as well, so that there is balance. But writing down what you feel, especially if there is no danger that anybody will read it, can be extremely therapeutic and will enable you to get your feelings out of your system to some extent.

You will also have a valuable permanent record of how you felt, and diary-keeping will enable you not to deny your feelings. When keeping a diary, never worry that recording what you really think may be embarrassing, or may reflect badly on you. Be honest, go with the feelings and don't be afraid of facing up to them.

As the diary proceeds, you will find writing down how you feel becomes easier and easier. If thoughts don't seem to flow, just write down what you did. Often, when reading back, you will find a surprising amount of emotion recorded there.

Writing certain things down will sometimes be painful. But you will feel better afterwards. Never worry about whether you are spelling words correctly, whether your grammar is up to scratch or whether you are any good at expressing yourself. Even a few simple lines will help – and having a record of the affair will help you to keep analysing it.

It's not necessary to write a diary entry every single day – just when emotions surge over. But if you keep it regularly, you will get into the habit. And when you read it back some time later you will discover how far you have come, how much progress you have made, and just how much you are understanding the situation.

One important DON'T: don't whatever you do, be tempted to show your diary entries to the object of your affections. This is the mistake that Kathleen Raine and Elizabeth Smart made with Gavin Maxwell and George Barker respectively – with dire results. Gavin Maxwell was horrified, believing that the diary entries would ruin his reputation if their contents ever became public, and George Barker simply did not understand the power of the passion Elizabeth Smart felt.

If you show the entries to your beloved they will very probably not be understood, and you may be seen as unhinged and dangerously over-emotional. Showing diary entries of agony and despair will not evoke loving feelings in the other person. You have no control over the other person's behaviour or feelings, and are powerless to alter or affect them. The only result may be even more alienation, as with Gavin Maxwell.

DO eat a good diet

This can be difficult at times of obsessive love. It is important to understand, though, that these feelings constitute a potent form of self-sabotage and that, in order to punish yourself even more, you may stop eating properly. But if you stuff, abstain, or over-indulge in empty carbohydrates, which simply make you feel worse, you will be adding to the stress. It is important to keep your blood sugar level constant, and to eat plenty of fresh fruit, fresh vegetables, brown rice, wholemeal bread — all the non-addictive foods. As obsessive love has much in common with an addiction, it cannot be helped or overcome by adding yet another addiction, that of over-eating — or deliberate under-eating.

DO keep off drugs

I'm not talking about illegal or street drugs here (although of course you should keep off those as well), but sleeping pills, anti-depressants or tranquillizers prescribed by the doctor. In extreme cases it may be necessary to take some kind of sedative to help over a temporary bad patch — this will be discussed in Chapter 6 — but never attempt to rely on any form of artificial anaesthetic to help you over an emotional crisis. All that will happen is that underneath the drug the effect of the obsession will get worse, and make eventual recovery even more difficult. For the same reason try not to drown your sorrows in alcohol — it only adds to the problem and increases the stress on your system.

DO talk to a friend

Don't be like Shakespeare's lady who sat like patience on a monument. If you can find a sympathetic friend to pour out your troubles to, this will help to get it all off your chest. It may seem that if you talk, try to analyse it or write a diary, doing so will somehow 'set' the obsession and make everything

90

worse. In fact it will be therapeutic and will ease the situation. There is probably, however, little point in a friend trying to offer concrete advice. It's best just to listen, to be sympathetic and non-judgemental, which can be extremely helpful at this time.

Sometimes friends may say they don't know what you see in this other person, or why you should find them so attractive. If you have a 'friend' like this, then stop confiding in this person. True friends will first agree that the beloved is extremely attractive, handsome and so on – and then try to get you to talk about what exactly you admire and appear to love. As obsessive love always happens when your self-esteem is particularly low, it is not helpful to be told that the object of your grand passion is somebody not worthy of you, not a worthy person at all. This just serves to make your self-esteem dive even lower.

In an ideal situation, of course, you should be able to talk things through with the beloved. But, given the obsession, given the possible indifference or callousness of the other person, this may not be possible at all.

See yourself as recovering from an illness. Don't be hard on yourself but take it, as they say in 'Anonymous' organizations, one day at a time.

DO cultivate other friendships

When we are obsessively in love, the tendency is to narrow everything down so that plenty of time is left free to be with the beloved or to think about this person. But make every attempt to widen your life out as much as possible: make new friends and develop new interests. That's not easy when all you want to do is to be with him/her – but it's essential to preserve your sanity. The trouble is that everything may seem horribly second-best; but remember that the more deliberate attempts you make to free yourself from the obsession, the more you are breaking the links in the chain that binds you to negative emotions.

If it's all in the past

But what if the obsession happened a long time ago? The white heat may have died down but you are left with a residue of resentment, hostility and, perhaps, a feeling that life has never gone quite right since the time of the fatal attraction.

● Understand and accept that you have been through a trauma. Don't make the mistake of thinking that because it happened a long time ago, or because it was not a big-scale devastation such as death or the loss of a limb, it is not important.

● Understand the importance of grieving − accepting fully the reality of the loss, acknowledging it, spending time feeling sad about it, rather than trying to cover up your feelings or pretending it never happened. Over the past few years the importance of grieving, or marking the end of anything which has been important, has at last been understood. The trouble with most obsessive relationships is that they never really finish. However long ago it's been, there may always lurk a hope in the back of one's mind that somehow it will all come right, and that you will meet up and be together. Accept that this is unlikely to happen, that this stage of your life is over; then mark it in some way, perhaps by writing or telephoning the former lover and seeing if you can meet up.

Meeting up in later life

This can prove excellent therapy − so long as you are meeting with love and benevolence and not any negative emotions. If you can, it will be helpful to talk through what happened all those years ago. You will probably find many surprises − perhaps that the beloved did not realize you were obsessed. He or she may have thought you hated them − a common interpretation of obsession.

You may also have thought that your lover hated you, as did the teenager writing in the *Guardian* (p 23). That, too, is unlikely. And, far from meeting a Casanova or a nymphomaniac, you will almost certainly find that this person is ordinary, fallible, nice, decent, full of doubts and fears − just like anybody else.

But if you do meet up, don't expect that true love will suddenly happen. You are a different person, the former beloved is a different person – and everything else is different too. You are probably no longer so vulnerable and self-conscious, but have grown in stature and maturity.

In maturity, you may be able to become friends. But it is much more likely that you will both see how little you have in common – and that the one meeting will just nicely finish off the formerly unfinished business.

But don't be tempted to meet if you want to show off, to prove to your former lover just how well you've done in spite of how badly you were treated. When emotions have not been worked through, there is often a desire for revenge. When, for instance, I was wondering whether I would ever meet John again, I had the feeling: I'll show him that, whatever he did to me, I've survived, been successful, had a fulfilling and exciting adult life. If feelings like this surface, don't give in to them – and don't meet. I don't think that meeting to 'even up the score' ever works – it may appear to make you feel better, but doesn't really touch the residue of negative emotions left by the affair; it may even fuel them.

If you're on the receiving end

If you are, or suspect that you are, on the receiving end of somebody's obsession, don't hope that it will just go away of its own accord. The more you try to ignore and evade it, the stronger the obsession will become.

The 'decent' thing would be to ask the besotted lover out to dinner, or for a drink or coffee, and then try to talk it all through. Explain that it is not the person but the fervent emotions which are being rejected, and that you know how he/she feels but you cannot return such a strong feeling. Be sympathetic and understanding, but don't agree to anything you don't want to do – such as going to bed with this person, going on holiday together or entering into any kind of exclusive relationship.

It's my belief that if those on the receiving end could bring themselves to talk, to be friendly, to be understanding, much of the misery now faced by besotted lovers would be minimized. The trauma could work itself out there and then, instead of being contained, perhaps for years.

Of coures, when people are obsessed in this way they are often not amenable to ordinary conversation and reasoning. The situation can be extremely frightening, especially when a woman is on the receiving end of a man's obsessive love. He may be violent and dangerous. If he or she seems completely unable to listen, the only real solution may be to remove yourself from this person's company. This is not always possible, of course − but when you are on the receiving end of somebody who has gone so badly out of control, always consider whether it is possible to remove yourself physically from them.

It may help to write to this person, explaining coolly that you appreciate the strength of their feelings for you, but that you cannot return them in the same way. Say that you have a high regard for the person, are impressed with their qualities and skills, but that a relationship such as they appear to be demanding is out of the question.

Don't feel flattered − many victims become nervous of obsessed lovers because they allow themselves to be flattered. This happens in almost every case of obsession, even where there is complete indifference. But the other person is not really obsessed by *you* − he or she is obsessed by an illusion which has sprung from their own dysfunction or problems. There is no real love and there never will be − which is why the obsession has to be treated with detachment and regard.

A major DON'T: don't go to bed with this person, or enter into any kind of sexual relationship in the belief that it may provide some kind of answer, or even because you feel 'turned on' by this person. When there is obsession the sex will be as obsessive, and for women it may be as frightening, as any other aspect of the problem. Of course it is tempting − especially in the early stages, the whole thing may seem heady and exciting, but it will never lead to the 'real thing'. Obsession can never turn into genuine love − and victims need to be aware of this.

In extreme cases consider asking for police protection, as Brigid (p 29 − 30) did. And certainly, whatever else you do, confide in somebody who may be in a position to help – the other person's doctor, parents, spouse, partner, boss at work. If you can't talk sensibly to the other person, because of their obsession, then somebody else might. It is most important to get somebody else to try and make them see what they are doing to you – and to understand that their feelings cannot be returned.

Don't attempt to keep it to yourself, or ever imagine you are to blame. Very many 'victims' of other people's obsession imagine that they have somehow caused it. This is not the case. But showing either indifference or fear merely serves to fuel the obsession. Victims mostly try to ignore it and pretend it's not happening, which is the very worst thing you can do.

It may be that in spite of all your efforts you are still obsessed with thoughts of your beloved, however unsatisfactory the relationship may be or has been. If this is so, you may like to consider professional help. But whatever the situation, never imagine that it *can't* be helped. And never believe that obsessive love is a trivial problem. If it were, would it have occupied the minds of so many great writers and thinkers since the beginning of recorded history?

6 Professional Help

Sometimes self-help measures may be enough to free you from the stranglehold of an obsessive relationship. But if the obsession has gone really deep, if it has lasted a very long time and just won't seem to go away, or if it all happened a long time ago but still impinges uncomfortably on your life, it may be worth considering some kind of therapy.

You don't have to be 'mad' or 'unhinged' to think about therapy or counselling. Just as we may need to call in a plumber to deal with a blocked drain, or an electrician to repair a wiring fault, so we may need help from an expert in unravelling the threads of the past and knitting them up together again harmoniously.

The right kind of professional therapy can help you to understand that you have been through a trauma which has left its mark on adult life, and which needs to be sorted out and faced before you can achieve true emotional health. Never try to minimize the effects of obsessive love, or imagine that it will all sort itself out in time.

Going for professional therapy can be extremely comforting. Friends may or may not understand what you have been through, but are rarely in a position to offer the kind of unconditional regard and acceptance which should be available from the right kind of therapist or counsellor.

Some people may be worried that if they go for therapy it means they are 'neurotic' and may be accused of dwelling on the past rather than wanting to get on with their lives. But being obsessive stops you from properly living in the present. It is only when you are able to acknowledge and bring out the pain of the past that you can let it go so that it will no longer affect you. Therapy may involve reliving and releasing the incident, as mine did. Or it may concentrate on bodily touch to release long-held emotions.

People are usually brought to therapy by feelings of low self-esteem. Although they may have achieved great personal success after an incident of obsessive love, they will often harbour residual lack of confidence, lack of esteem, and all the feelings of blame, denial and shame discussed earlier. Successful therapy will enable these feelings to be sorted out and examined – and the psyche to be healed.

Only you can tell when the time may be right for some kind of professional help – usually that time comes when you feel strongly that you want to deal with it and are capable of dealing with it. Sometimes the pain is so great and the aftermath so shocking that everything is numbed for years afterwards.

Nowadays there are very many kinds of professional help available – and no reputable therapist will judge you harshly for having gone out of control with a long-ago love affair. The reality of your experience will be accepted and worked through.

But how can you tell whether you may find therapy or some other form of recognized treatment helpful? Here are some indications:

1. If ever you have loved and lost and still feel hurt, grief, despair many years after the event, or if you cannot, however hard you try, get somebody completely out of your mind, you may well be suffering from the after-effects of the phenomenon.

2. If you feel you could cheerfully kill your former lover if ever you set eyes on him/her again, you are still negatively attached and may need to take specific steps to untie the remaining knot and release the ancient feelings.

3. If you have got into the habit of feeling resentful and hostile towards this person, even if you have not had any active relationship for many years, it would be helpful to try to remove this habit.

97

4. If you have a suspicion that not everything is right with your life, that there is some deep-seated inability to form proper relationships or that your adult relationships since the disastrous affair have never gone quite right, or unaccountably don't last or seem mysteriously sabotaged – then you may be in the grip of lingering suffering from a much earlier, unsatisfactory and one-sided relationship.

   More than anything else, the after-effect of an obsessive, passionate involvement with somebody is that you can no longer trust your feelings, that you have lost the ability to empathize and feel connected to other humans. This tends to happen after any kind of abuse – sexual abuse, emotional abuse, incest or being beaten as a child. Some ability to feel is forever afterwards shut off, so that perhaps you seem cold and hard, unfeeling – completely logical, like Mr Spock in *Star Trek*.

5. If you now feel that all men (or all women) are not to be trusted, are shallow worthless deceivers and will always treat you badly, you may well still be suffering from shock.

6. If your former beloved seems to return to you in dreams, this may be an indication that it's time to deal with the incident. For about a year before I finally decided to get to the bottom of it I kept having dreams about John which were so vivid that they woke me up. I remembered them so well that I wrote them down. In the dreams he was impossibly handsome and loving and we had a blissful relationship – so much so that I did not want to believe it was a dream. Nothing like this, of course, had happened in real life – but there was nothing I could do to prevent the dreams or alter them.

   The dreams could have been coded messages to me to try to understand this disturbance – I don't know. I do know that since therapy I have not had a single dream about him. What we try to stop coming through to the conscious mind often has a habit of reminding us of its existence when we are unconscious.

7.   If you never seem to be really well, are suffering from a depleted immune system – and there has been an obsessive relationship in your past – then the two may be connected.

Why professional help may be needed

Over time, the feelings and emotions outlined above can, like anything else, become habits of thought which eventually get so ingrained that you may be tempted to believe: this is me, this is what I am like. Sayings such as, 'I've got a short fuse', 'I flare up easily', 'I've got a short temper', and 'I'm easily hurt' belong to old scripts which relate to some terrible hurt or abuse in the past.

Obsessive love does, of course, constitute abuse and a severe shock to the system, resulting in stress, anxiety and tension. Many modern therapies, recognizing that problems in life can often be traced back to a traumatic event, attempt to strip away the tarnish of negative emotions so that one is left with the silver of oneself.

Old, outdated habits of thought can easily become self-fulfilling prophecies which prevent the true personality from showing through. An incident of obsessive love can warp the personality until the hurt that it caused can be released. And the longer the emotion has been allowed to fester, the more likely it is that skilled help will be needed as it has become embedded deep in the system.

All long-held hurts, hostilities and resentments constitute mental stress which adversely affect the personality. All over-indulgence in alcohol, gambling, addictive drugs, shopping or eating are ways that we may try to plaster over the emotional hurt. In many cases the affair itself may be consciously forgotten as the mind tries to protect itself by cloaking unpleasant incidents with comforting amnesia – at least for a time.

It seems clear, from research carried out so far, that obsession springs from some internal, deeply felt need rather than anything which comes from the loved one. Rarely does the object of the obsession feel that here is true love which should be gratefully harnessed and returned. As one of our case histories in Chapter 2, Brigid, remarked about her fifty-year-old lover who would not leave her alone: 'I never doubted that he loved me. But it didn't feel like love. You end up confused and you simply don't understand what it is. There is too much discomfort for it to feel like love.'

Wrong advice

In the past, the standard advice from professionals such as doctors and psychiatrists was to pull yourself together and forget all about him or her. If only we could! Now it is increasingly being realized that both are impossible: sufferers are caught in the grip of something they cannot easily control, and as for forgetting − well, advice to stop breathing might be easier to take. But don't imagine that professional help has to be big-time, years-long analysis. Often a small number of sessions will be enough − so long as they are with the right person.

There is also a school of thought which says let the past stay in the past. Our present society has been very good at not admitting the pains of the past and trying not to allow them to come to the surface. It was this attitude which resulted in the 'stiff upper lip' mentality which may once have enabled us to win empires and keep the natives down, but which is not serving us very well now.

Whenever attempts are made to block off trauma the effect is the same: denial, freezing of emotions, blaming others. In an attempt to escape our own pain we become not entirely human.

How can we tell whether an event has been traumatic?

Past traumas have a habit of forcing their way to the surface sooner or later, although not always in ways that seem obvious.

The biggest clue to the presence of a deep-seated trauma is

some highly inappropriate emotional reaction to an everyday event – something which unaccountably evokes a memory or calls up highly disturbing feelings or emotions. The trigger for me was when I was walking in my garden with my former boyfriend (p 16). Although I had no idea that the affair with John was the cause, I could not understand why I should have such disturbing feelings – especially in relation to somebody with whom I had never had a disturbing relationship in the past.

Another clue is if you have extremely strong personal reactions to something which should not deeply affect you. Anybody who feels personal rage when reading a story of obsessive love, or who feels enormous anger towards a complete stranger who has not returned passionate love, should ask themselves *why* they feel such anger and rage.

We only ever feel outraged when something inside us is deeply touched. To give another example – for years Neville, my former husband, used to feel personal, blinding rage when he heard of babies being bottle-fed. Although we all know that breast-feeding is best, most people do not feel personally insulted when reading about bottle-feeding. But Neville did. He though at the time it was righteous anger – but learned later that he was giving vent to personal rage about being bottle-fed himself.

It is also possible that, when there has been severe trauma, emotions are blocked to such a great extent that we do not feel pity, sympathy and empathy when we ought to. Child psychologist Alice Miller has drawn attention to the way in which very many adults do not ever empathize with their children's pain, but cause them terrible emotional or physical hurt.

The reason for this, she says, is always that the adults have experienced similar terrible pain themselves. It has been so bad that they have introjected – blamed themselves for causing their parents distress – and have told themselves that if they were severely punished they must have deserved it, as parents always want the best for their child.

Anybody, says Alice Miller, who treats children or animals badly, and who does not seem to feel remorse or guilt or to have any idea of what the child might be suffering, has blocked off their own pain so much that they have become incapable of empathizing with others. This is how society gets torturers and terrible dictators, she believes.

If we experienced a shameful, distressing incident of obsessive love, it is very possible that we may lose all feelings for others who might be going through something similar. If we feel nothing at all when we hear such stories, it may be that we have blocked off our own pain in similar circumstances.

Sometimes the trauma of obsessive love may be recalled quite by accident, when you are least expecting it. Meditation has become extremely popular in the West over the past twenty years or so, and nowadays more people than ever are meditating regularly. One of the things that meditation does is to still the mind, so that unpleasant incidents from the past, apparently deeply buried, may rise up of their own accord. For no apparent reason, a memory may suddenly surface.

This is your indication that it's time to do something about it, to go with the memory rather than try to push it down again. Only you can tell when it might be time to deal with the problems of the past. But usually, they won't go away of their own accord.

Here are some therapies and techniques which may be helpful in releasing the trauma, and enable you to face life free from its influence. The first of them are physical rather than psychological, and it may seem odd at first that these purely physical therapies can activate memories of ancient emotional problems. You first have to accept the possibility that emotional problems can be held in the physical body, even when the conscious memory of these has long since disappeared. We speak, for instance, of people being 'bowed' with grief, or 'weighed down' with sorrow. Anybody interested in the physical therapies outlined below should be prepared for memories to surface – they may not, but it is not always possible to predict when they will.

The Alexander Technique

This is primarily a physical therapy: the Alexander teacher asks the pupil to sit, stand and walk properly – that is, in the way that our bodies were meant to before they got into bad habits. Mostly it is some physical distress, such as chronic lower back pain, migraine or arthritis, which persuades people to seek out Alexander teachers, and only rarely will they probe into emotional problems. However, when therapy is under way correction of a bad physical or postural habit will often activate some deeply buried memory and result in floods of tears or other manifestation of deep anguish when it is brought to the surface.

Alexander teachers believe that past emotional wounds can often be healed simply by working on the physical body; and, of course, obsessive love constitutes an emotional wound of a particularly searing nature. The nature of the technique will allow long-held emotions to be released, but this may not happen all at once. Often, people may go for ten or more lessons before the real reason for the bad posture, the physical problems, is revealed. Frequently, though, a technique such as the Alexander will act as a stepping-stone to other kinds of therapies which access and heal the specific wound.

So what actually happens at an Alexander lesson? You do not have to wear special clothes or take anything off. Most lessons are held on a one-to-one basis, so there is no competitive aspect. You don't have to worry about what other people are thinking or feeling, and the teacher is concentrating entirely on you.

During the first lesson the teacher will explain what the Alexander Technique is all about and teach you how to use your body in more efficient and healthy ways. All lessons are focused on the individual, which is why a detailed case history is often taken at the start. The teacher will want to know what your health problems are, and whether you have had any serious illnesses in the past. She will not ask about emotional traumas, although all Alexander teachers know that both physical and emotional traumas are often held in the body for years. She will then probably ask why you have come, and what you hope to gain from an Alexander session.

A warning will be given that the technique is not a magic cure-all for every single disease or emotional problem – but that it can always help. Alexander teachers never concentrate, though, on illness or negativity. They always ask people to do things as if they were in full health and strength, and make no allowances for backache, migraine or arthritis, for example. This allows them to ascertain just what is wrong, by observing which actions the pupil is unable to perform or for any reason finds difficult.

Alexander teachers also understand that some people seem to 'need' their illnesses or emotional problems, and would feel lost without them. Above all, the technique emphasizes the overwhelming influence of habit. F. Matthias Alexander, the Australian actor who first developed the technique, believed that we can never underestimate the strength of habit.

Any action and any thought, he said, if repeated often enough goes from the conscious into the unconscious, by which time we are not even aware that we have the habit, so much a part of us has it become. He believed that stammering, for example, was a habit. The reason people found it such a difficult habit to break was that they were speaking all the time, so they never got the opportunity to break the link.

It is the same with habits of thought. Over the years they become so ingrained that we are not even aware that they are habits. The Alexander Technique is primarily concerned with unlearning bad habits, rather than learning new ones. Its main aim is to help people get back into equilibrium – and as we so often hold emotional traumas in the body, correcting the body can have the effect of releasing the emotional problem as well.

All reputable Alexander teachers will try to find out why the pupil has come, whether there is a willingness to learn, and what the pupil's attitude to himself or herself is. Any deep-seated panic or anxiety will be noted, as teachers closely observe the body language of their pupils.

After about fifteen minutes of consulation the actual lesson begins. This consists of lying on a special table with knees bent and the head resting on a pile of two or three books, so that the spine lies straight on the table. The Alexander teacher then lifts up your head, arms and legs in turn, asking you to 'give her the weight' – not to make any attempt to help her. She wants people to be 'deadweights' so that she can search out where the imbalances are.

The more tense and nervous people are, the less able they are to give the teacher the weight. They are afraid of 'surrendering' up to somebody who at this stage is still a stranger. For some people, just learning to let the teacher take the weight can take several lessons.

After this is done the teacher will move round the body, touching muscles in strategic places. There is no pain, no discomfort or difficulty while this is taking place, and the pupil may find it hard to believe that anything is happening. What the teacher is doing at this stage is finding out how your muscles are positioned, what you have been doing to your spine and where the problem areas might be.

The teacher will then ask the pupil to let the neck muscles soften and release. After this, you will be asked to get off the table in a special way, by rolling on to one side and gradually lowering your legs on to the floor. After this you may be asked to stand with your back against the back of a chair, and to sit in the Alexander way. The teacher 'sits' you, observing the realtionship of your head to your spine, and seeing how far out of alignment it is.

The first consultation takes about an hour, and often nothing very much appears to have happened. But next day you may be aware of all kinds of peculiar aches and pains. You may also be asked to do some homework – lying down in the Alexander way, perfectly still, with your head on books, for about fifteen minutes. Most people find this surprisingly difficult.

As the lessons go on, and your posture and alignment become corrected, long-held emotional problems may be released. Some people break down in floods of tears as they remember something they had long ago consciously forgotten. One pupil who went for Alexander lessons for backache suddenly started crying uncontrollably as she remembered, for the first time in many years, the agony she felt at the age of six when her parents got divorced.

What the Alexander Technique teaches above all is that we can, if we want to, be in control of our minds and bodies. We can choose good posture, correct body use and positive thinking – or we can do the opposite and choose bad posture and go around with minds full of negative thoughts. For many people, going for Alexander lessons is the first step towards healing and personal growth.

Massage

Like the Alexander Technique, massage is of course mainly a physical therapy; but again it can often be the first step to recognizing and releasing an ancient trauma. The point about massage is that you have to trust the therapist completely – you are literally in her hands, and many people find even this level of trust difficult.

For many years massage was considered a kind of self-indulgence, something vaguely pleasant but not of much use therapeutically. Now, though, massage is being used increasingly in hospitals, and for seriously and terminally ill people as a potent healing tool. It has proved particularly beneficial for heart patients.

Very often, when somebody has been traumatized by obsessive love there is a kind of shutting-down of responses, which may include physical ones. If you allow yourself to be massaged, this can be a way of getting back in touch with your feelings. The main aim of therapeutic massage is relaxation – something most of us find surprisingly difficult. People often choose to have massage when they are feeling particularly low or tense, and want to feel better.

In good hands, you cannot help but feel better. You are being touched in a loving yet detached and non-sexual way; and gradually, as the massage proceeds, you will find that muscles relax and your mind eases up too. Most massage therapists are female, although there are now excellent male masseurs. They tend to have stronger hands, but the touch may be less gentle – it depends what you are looking for. Some people prefer tough massage, while others like to be stroked gently. The masseuse may also use aromatherapy oils, which help the therapeutic process and can aid relaxation.

Rolfing

This is a particular type of connective tissue manipulation which is much stronger than ordinary massage, and may even be quite painful at first. Its founder, Dr Ida Rolf, believed, like Alexander, that feelings long held in the body can create physical changes and damage. As with the Alexander Technique, Rolfing often involves release of emotional pain, even though the technique works purely on the physical body. Memories of past traumatic events are often recalled as the therapist works on different parts of the body.

Rolfing sessions last for about an hour, and patients usually go once a week. You will be photographed from all sides to enable you to monitor your progress and see yourself 'before' and 'after'. The therapist uses her knuckles and fingers to stretch and separate layers of connective tissue. She will then work on the abdomen, ribcage, pelvis, feet and even the inside of the mouth. Some people find Rolfing extremely pleasurable, while others experience quite intense pain. The more 'knotted up' you are the more likely you are to experience pain, although it is only momentary.

Again, as with ordinary massage and the Alexander Technique, Rolfing is usually seen as a method of personal growth; it is an important step towards healing and realization of potential.

As these therapies are all quite intimate – massage and Rolfing do involve taking off clothes, even though Alexander lessons do not – it is essential for trust and rapport to be built up between therapist and client. If, for any reason, you do not feel happy or secure with your teacher or masseuse, don't continue with the lessons; they could do more harm than good. The whole point of all these therapies is that they should be enjoyable and you should feel very different after them.

Circle dancing

At first this may sound a strange kind of therapy, but circle dancing, which in its present form began life in the early 1980s, is now increasingly being used as a therapeutic tool. It is a form of dance, closely connected to ancient ritual, where people get into a circle, hold hands and execute a number of simple steps in time to music. The point about circle dancing is that it is non-competitive and non-patriarchal (unlike ballroom dancing, where men lead and women follow); everybody is equal.

There are now circle dancing groups in most parts of the UK, in Europe and America. The idea is that through group dynamics, the movement and energies released through dancing together, long-held problems can come to the surface and be released. The act of dancing in this way, with other people, is actually healing.

Although some people use circle dancing for relaxation, enjoyment and exercise, most find that they definitely get something more from the experience as they keep going. As explained earlier, one of the after-effects of obsessive love (or any serious trauma, come to that) is that the experience cuts you off from relating properly to other people. By connecting to other people in this harmless way, a sense of relatedness can be re-established. Circle dancing helps people to remember that they are part of a community, part of the whole, and have much in common with everybody else.

Circle dancing sessions last for about an hour and a half, and several different dances will be enacted. It doesn't matter if you do the wrong steps – nobody will be judging you. The sessions are always led by a circle dancing expert, and nowadays there are people who specialize in running such groups.

People who would love to be able to dance, but who have always been nervous of ballroom dancing, often find that circle dancing provides just the release they need. For many people, attending circle dancing sessions enables them to get back in touch with themselves, or at least with a part of themselves that may seem to have vanished.

It is essential to go to an expert for sessions – the steps are very specific, and all have ancient meanings.

Autogenic training

This technique was developed in the 1930s as a method of meditation for Westerners. It basically teaches people how to switch off the 'fight or flight' mechanism in their bodies which leads to fear and anxiety and increased stress, and how to switch on the rest, relaxation and recreation system.

As with the Alexander Technique and circle dancing, autogenic training is not a self-help measure and has to be taught by a qualified teacher. The reason is that many people experience peculiar reactions, known as abreactions, when undergoing autogenic training. Repressed emotions start to come out and are released in the form of uncontrollable tears, laughter or even moments of pain. If you attempt to do the exercises yourself you may not be prepared for the release of emotions – but the therapist will be on the lookout for them.

The training, a mixture of autosuggestion and autohypnotism, consists of a series of exercises designed to promote 'passive concentration'. Patients are taught how to relax every part of their body in turn by giving themselves instructions such as: 'My right arm feels heavy', and 'My left leg feels warm.'

Most courses consist of eight sessions, by which time you will have learnt the technique well enough to be able to do it on your own. Autogenics can be practised anywhere – when driving a car, just before a job interview, or during any nerve-racking experience. It is a conscious, controlled form of relaxation and, like the Alexander Technique, is designed to bring unconscious and unhelpful habits into conscious control.

Many people find that autogenics helps by enabling them to know themselves better through relaxation. The technique actually demands quite a lot of concentration, and can be considered a form of meditation. It is frequently the first step in getting to know yourself, taking time out for yourself and realizing that you are important.

Very often, where there has been an incident of obsessive love in the past which has left a memory of having been spurned and rejected, there are feelings of worthlessness and low self-esteem. Although autogenics may sound simple, it can have profound effects. It is basically a way of getting back in touch with yourself – as all these physical therapies are.

In recent years autogenic training has been subjected to a great deal of clinical research, and has proved itself a reliable technique for promoting relaxation and releasing stress. But like any other therapy it must be practised regularly if it is to have any effect.

Hatha yoga

The ancient art of tying yourself up in knots, known as hatha yoga, has also recently undergone a number of clinical trials in hospitals. It is proving effective in the release of very many psychosomatic complaints.

There are two main aspects to hatha yoga – pranayama (breathing) and asanas (postures). The therapeutic value of going to yoga classes is that during the session it is impossible to think of anything else except the breathing or physical postures.

Yoga demands great concentration and is usually conducted in a class with severeal other pupils, but it is emphatically not competitive. You are not even competing with yourself or trying to achieve a 'personal best', although of course you will improve with regular practice. It is of course perfectly possible to do yoga on one's own, but the greatest benefits come from attending a class, where group dynamics operate. You will find, too, that you are stretched and challenged more when in a class – there is a great temptation to cheat on one's own; and, to tell the truth, doing yoga on one's own is extremely boring.

Anybody at all, of any age or fitness level, should be able to find a suitable yoga class these days. People often find they gain in self-confidence when going to classes, as progress can be sudden and startling. Most yoga teachers and organizations hold classes for beginners, intermediate and advanced pupils. Although there are several different schools of yoga, most follow a basic pattern throughout the class.

You have to wear loose-fitting trousers and top, leotard and leggings or a track suit – not jeans. The class usually starts with fifteen to twenty minutes of pranayama, which has the effect of expelling stale air and clearing out the lungs. Then comes the sun salutation – the most famous yoga posture, and one designed to get every part of the body moving.

After that come the asanas, starting usually with the head-stand. The thought of this often makes people nervous and they imagine they can never do it themselves. Most people find, though, that within a very few weeks they can do the headstand perfectly. Then comes the shoulderstand.

Yoga classes are designed so that each posture has its counterposture, and thus each part of the body is systematically exercised. After the inverted postures – headstand and shoulderstand – come a series of forward bends.

You will then lie on your abdomen and execute backward bends – always doing counterpostures after each asana. Usually there will be a brief period of relaxation between each set of postures. Finally you will do spinal twists and standing-up exercises. The more advanced you become, the longer you will be able to hold each posture – and it is in the holding of postures that the greatest benefit is gained.

Yoga is not an endurance test, and nobody should do exercises to the point of pain. But by gradually stretching yourself you will find you can do things you never even thought possible, such as the lotus position, the wheel (known in children's playgrounds as the crab) and the crow, where you go down on all fours, then balance on your hands only, with your knees supported by your elbows.

Classes usually end with ten to fifteen minutes of 'final relaxation', where you relax every part of your body, including the internal organs, in turn. When people first go for yoga classes, they may find that the final relaxation is the most difficult part of all, as that is the time when unwelcome thoughts can come into the mind. For ages, when I first went to yoga classes, worries about money kept churning in my head as I was supposed to be relaxing. Needless to say, worry and relaxation do not go together.

Some people are actually frightened of the final relaxation sessions. But in time, relaxation will become possible. The reason that unwelcome or worrying thoughts often come into the head when we are trying consciously to relax is that most of us do our utmost to make sure that these thoughts *don't* enter. We subject ourselves to constant stimulation – television, radio, dinners out, socializing, workaholism – all to suppress the thoughts that are threatening to rise up. It

111

is frequently only when we are prepared to 'go with' these thoughts, to try to access aspects of ourselves which we may have buried, that we may consider one of the therapies outlined here.

Although it is possible to learn yoga from a book, the greatest benefits come when it is taught by a dedicated teacher. As with autogenic training, clinical trials are now being conducted into yoga. It is being found that the asanas can be extremely helpful for a number of psychosomatic complaints, and also for those who are greatly troubled by worry and stress of any kind.

Meditation

This is often the next step on from autogenic training and yoga, which both provide a kind of introduction to meditation. The 'passive concentration' which autogenic training teaches is in itself a form of meditation, while most yoga classes end with a short meditation and a prayer.

Meditation can be described as the art of stilling the mind and turning it inwards, to bring about inner peace and achieve introspection. It has become extremely popular in the West since the 1960s, when it was introduced here from the East.

Some people take to meditation instantly, while others find it extremely difficult, if not impossible. As a general rule, the more extrovert you are the more difficult you are likely to find it. The stillness, the attempt to focus thoughts, can be extremely unnerving. Also, as in yoga, unwelcome thoughts can rise to the surface when you least want them.

There are very many schools of meditation, ranging from those which appear to be purely for relaxation to those which are extremely spiritual and may seem weird to the newcomer. The best-known method of meditation in the West is TM – Transcendental Meditation – but there are now many others, most of which have an Eastern guru of some kind somewhere in the background or foreground.

But beware: although all kinds of meditation may sound superficially the same, and many are now heavily advertised, some schools of meditation are out to get your money or to encourage you to sign up for expensive courses. As a general rule, avoid any meditation organization which asks you to hand over large sums of money – £100 or more for a day or weekend course. As a rule of thumb, the cheaper the meditation courses are, the more likely they are to be genuine. Reputable methods and schools are included in the Resources section on page 144. Unfortunately, offering meditation classes is often a way of sucking unsuspecting people into dangerous cults – which doesn't mean that meditation itself is dangerous, of course.

After initial experience in a group it becomes easy enough to practise meditation on your own. The best position is sitting cross-legged (known in hatha yoga as the 'easy' posture) with your hands either on your knees or lightly touching at your groin. The point about this posture is that it keeps all your body energy contained in one place, and does not allow it to dissipate. Your back should be straight. If you can't easily sit cross-legged on the floor, use a cushion. Ideally your knees should be on the floor, but this takes a lot of practice for most people.

Then do what feels best for you. Some people prefer to meditate with their eyes closed, others with them open. If your eyes are open, concentrate on something within the room. It may help to have an incense stick burning; some meditation experts advocate silently chanting a sound such as 'Om' to help the mind to focus. The point about the silent chanting is that it helps the mind to concentrate and be still, rather than to think about tomorrow's shopping, work or relationships. These sounds are known as mantras, and they are supposed to have special vibrations. 'Om' is the commonest and simplest mantra, but others frequently used are 'Om Namah Sivaya' or 'Om Namo Narayanaya' – invocations to gods in the Hindu pantheon.

Some schools of meditation have replaced ancient Hindu mantras with a more Western sound, such as 'Ah'. This is because people new to meditation can find these Hindu sounds off-putting, alien and redolent of the hippy sixties.

Some people find it helpful to meditate to a special commentary – many tapes are available to aid meditation. Others like listening to suitable 'New Age' music – sounds of waves or birdsong, for example.

Try to sit like this for fifteen minutes a day. If something is

113

deeply bothering you, you will find that eventually it rises up. Usually, people who hate meditation are those who cannot cope with the unwelcome thoughts that come into their minds – sometimes those of bitter hatred, rather than of peace and love, which is what we are supposed to be thinking about.

The thing is to go with the thought, not to try to suppress it. Ask yourself why it has come up and what you can do to deal with it. Practising meditation frees the mind, so that these thoughts will rise up. Sometimes, unaccountably, you will feel angry or full of rage. As meditation proceeds, different layers of the mind will come to the surface.

One teacher described meditation as rather like cleaning an extremely tarnished brass item. When you first start to rub, amazing amounts of dirt come off, but the item never seems to get cleaner. In fact, it gets worse at first. But as you keep rubbing, gradually the shine starts to emerge – and you are rewarded for your efforts.

The whole point of meditation is to strip away 'dirty' layers of the mind, so that the real you – the positive, loving you – comes through. There is nothing to be afraid of, even if you do experience unaccountable bouts of anger and disturbance – these are signs that the process is beginning to work.

Never be nervous when some long-buried memory starts to surface – this is a clear sign that you are ready to deal with it and to release it. There is a saying: what we can't feel, we can't heal.

It is usually when we can't feel pain that it continues to do harm: rather like cancer, which in its early stages is completely painless and unnoticed. But, unlike some forms of cancer, emotional pain can almost always be healed – if we are willing to let it.

Psychotherapy and counselling

Memories activated by meditation, yoga or any other physical therapy may be simply too traumatic to be dealt with on one's own. Sometimes prolonged meditation will have the requisite healing effect, but not always. 'Healing' in this sense happens when there are no longer any thoughts of anger, fear or obsession towards another person. But if such thoughts continue to trouble you, more formal therapy may well be needed before they can be released for ever.

Psychotherapy and counselling are both rather vague terms which are now rapidly seeping into everyday language. The situation at the moment is that anybody can set up as a psychotherapist or counsellor without having any qualifications or training. And wrong or inappropriate psychotherapy may well do more harm than good.

Although recognized training does not mean that the therapist is guaranteed to help you, and conversely lack of formal training does not mean that the therapist is no good, it is necessary to be on your guard. If possible, go on personal recommendation rather than replying to advertisements in newspapers or magazines. No therapist or counsellor who is reputable ever needs to advertise.

But personal recommendation is not everything. The most important aspect of all is to feel a strong rapport with the counsellor, that he or she knows exactly what to do to make you feel at ease and as if you are in a safe place. If you have any doubts at all, even though the therapist may seem perfectly good and genuine, it might be better not to proceed. Ask for an introductory session before committing yourself to a full course, which can be extremely expensive.

Although there are many different schools of psychotherapy and counselling, most therapists will proceed by asking a series of questions to try to discover exactly what your problem is. But always you will tell them — they won't put thoughts into your head. If this happens don't proceed with the therapy, as it could be dangerous.

Depending on the type of therapy you choose you may be sitting in a chair or lying on a couch. As a general rule, psychotherapy proceeds with the patient lying on a couch, while with counselling the client is sitting on a chair facing the therapist.

In Britain, psychotherapy is usually defined as a method of dealing with general problems, whereas counselling is meant to help with something specific. But in practice the terms are interchangeable, and nobody has really arrived at a satisfactory separation of the two. In America, what we would call counselling is usually known as psychotherapy.

There are now many therapists specializing in trauma counselling — that it, helping people to come to terms with a specific terrible problem in their lives. Although the methods used vary, the idea is that the client will be asked to relive the experience so that it can be brought into the conscious mind, and then released with understanding and knowledge. Hypnosis is not usually used, although there will be an altered state of consciousness, a deeper or different state of awareness, as therapy proceeds.

You, as the client, will know when and if you and the therapist combined 'hit the spot'. Sometimes, in spite of good intentions on both sides, that spot is not hit. This can mean one of two things: either that the therapist is barking up completely the wrong tree, or that it is not time for you to deal with this problem.

A good therapist, though, should not mislead, as everything ought to come from you as the client. The therapist should not ask leading questions, but reflect what you have said, at the same time helping you to move on so that the emotional hurt comes to the surface.

Regression therapy

This is the most helpful kind to deal with past incidents of obsessive love, so look for somebody who specializes in this kind of treatment. Regression therapists have been trained to ask the kind of questions which will activate past memories, and then help you to get through them.

Very often, when there has been a traumatic incident in the past, the experience has never been properly 'lived through'. What happens is that people tend to shut down, even while it is happening, and say to themselves: 'This is not taking place. I am not experiencing it.' This is particularly common with victims of child sexual abuse, who have shut off the pain so much that they cannot remember anything at all about the event.

Often, a period of amnesia at a time when there should be memory is a clue to the therapist that here is something that has been shut off. We do so to enable ourselves to survive the hurt – but as we have already seen, it is often at a great cost. In adult life, or in later years, the mechanism which helped us to survive the trauma can be extremely unhelpful. This is why it needs to be replaced by something more positive and healing for us.

Many adults who have been severely abused as children cannot remember anything from the ages of seven to eleven, for example – a time which ought to be full of conscious memories. Those who have suffered from obsessive love may have a complete blank of the years between eighteen and twenty, for instance – it's as if they have been completely wiped off the slate. But underneath the surface, of course, the memories are still extremely potent. They have simply been tranquillized rather than excised.

For regression therapy you will most probably be lying down, covered with a blanket, while the therapist sits beside you. He or she may say a few words to help you get into a relaxed state, and may use crystals or music at the start. The therapy room itself should be warm and peaceful, with no distractions at all.

A tape recorder may be used. It is extremely helpful to tape sessions, because very often you simply don't remember what you are saying; the real impact may hit you only when listening to the tape. In addition, it is extremely helpful afterwards to have a recording of what happened at the session, so that your progress can be monitored.

Most regression therapists take longer than the 'fifty-minute hour' of standard psychotherapists and counsellors. This is because it is often difficult to access buried memories, and there may be long periods of silence followed by recollections of nothing very much. When there has been serious trauma, an hour may not be long enough to start to get anywhere, as so much resistance is often encountered. You may find there is resistance, or you may find it comes pouring out – either way you have to proceed at your own pace, and the therapist will respect this.

Usually, the therapy leads up to the period of obsessive love, rather than starting with it. Most therapists want to put it into context, to be able to relate it to childhood experiences and emotions. Very often, those who fall prey to obsessive love are people who considered themselves special and different as children, who did not seem to fit into their surroundings and always thought of themselves as 'better' in some ways than their families.

This superior attitude, in itself a means of survival, of not relating, is probably the greatest single personality characteristic which leads to obsessive love. But beware of any therapist who tries to pigeonhole you – as mentioned before, all the information should come from you rather than being suggested by the therapist. Remember that, although there are now many theories about certain childhood experiences contributing to adult problems, they remain theories – they are not set in concrete, and they may not apply to you.

When you and the therapist feel that the moment has arrived, the moment when you will begin to relive the experience, the questions will become more specific. You will very likely feel a knot in your stomach, or you may weep or show some other strong emotional reaction that you will probably not be able to control. Don't worry about this – the therapist is entirely used to such outbursts and will notice them as being significant. Don't worry, either, if you can't remember everything. You will find that as you continue memories will flood back.

Psychotherapist Vera Diamond, who specializes in regression therapy, says:

> *The reason it is so vitally important to excise troubled memories from the past is that, until we do, we cannot properly live in the present. The only way we can properly live in the present, be a hundred per cent ourselves, is if we can shed the trauma, open that locked door, have the courage to face up to what really happened, and relive it.*
>
> *We have to pass through the fear barrier which is, basically, a fear of ourselves, of our own reactions.*

There will often be blame, recriminations, feelings of guilt, a wish that a better light could be shed on the whole sorry episode. No good therapist, though, will be judgemental – whatever you may have done, or however bad you may feel about yourself for succumbing to this passion, there will always be complete acceptance of what you have done.

As the session proceeds you will be asked to recall the event as if you were experiencing it now – as if you were being asked to describe a movie while watching it. And this is exactly what it feels like. A kind of screen will unfold in front of your eyes, and you will see your one-time lover, not as he (or she) is now, but as they were then. You will again feel all the strength of the impact you felt when you first saw this person, first became obsessed. Every emotion you went through then will flood back, and you will go back in time to when you were that age. You will forget that you are now a sensible, sober, adult person – and you will become again that obsessed, haunted, powerless, out-of-control individual.

Everything will come back in super-strength, and it's as if there has been no intervening time. You will surprise yourself by remembering things you thought you had long forgotten, or which you never even realized had registered. There will be enormous clarity as the therapy proceeds, and you will feel exactly as you felt then.

A good therapist will attempt to heal all the time, and help you put it all into context. She will help you to see that you were powerless to prevent whatever happened at the time. She will also help you to see that you were not to blame, and that you were incapable of affecting the other person's emotions. You could not, whatever you tried to do, make that person love you. Nor were you responsible for his (or her) behaviour. The way that the other person behaved was their responsibility, not yours.

The therapist will help you not to judge yourself harshly for how you behaved, not to feel terrible remorse or, alternatively, to hate or blame the other person. What happened happened. Nothing can make it unhappen, but amends can be made, the knot untied and the hurt healed.

The therapy we are talking about here is not long-time psychoanalysis, but should be complete within three or four sessions. Obviously, the more disturbed you were by the incident, the more sessions will be needed, but usually it will not take all that long to get it out of your system once you have made up your mind to deal with the problem.

If the therapy has been successful, you will be amazed at

the results. You will, for the first time, feel clarity, clean-liness, and as if you have shed a massive burden. There will also be a feeling that you can face the future with confidence, that there is no longer any need for this burden from the past to affect you. Successful therapy will also be marked by a dramatic change of attitude towards the other person. All the pent-up hate and resentment will vanish and should be replaced by feelings of love and benevolence.

Sometimes, it may be helpful to contact the other person again, as I did, to release any lingering attachment. Only you can decide this. Some people are nervous that they may fall desperately in love all over again, and it will all be just as hopeless. I would say this is unlikely after therapy, although it could well happen before.

Other people may be worried that they will wonder what-ever they first saw in this person – and this may make them doubly ashamed. Again, I would say that if there has been great intensity, this is unlikely. Although the other person may have changed – may not be young and good-looking any more, and may not have turned out the way you expected – there will usually be 'something' there that makes you think: yes, he/she *is* unusual, attractive, indi-vidual.

The best that can happen, if you do meet again, is that you will find you have things in common, establish a rapport and become friends. At the very least you will meet, wish each other well, talk and laugh over the incident and then go your separate ways.

By meeting up you may also discover that you had quite a wrong impression of your former lover. You may have considered this person particularly glamorous, confident, in control – but they may confess to seeing themselves as shy, awkward and nervous.

Regression therapy is becoming extremely popular, as it is increasingly being understood how therapeutic it is to shed dark secrets from the past and become liberated from them – whatever those dark secrets may be. Although most regression therapists specialize in helping victims of child abuse, don't imagine that you have to have suffered as a child to benefit. Abuse can happen at any age – and it always leaves a scar.

Co-counselling

Another type of therapy which may be just as helpful is known as co-counselling. This is a non-authoritarian method of counselling, where the same person can be both counsellor and client. Here, instead of going to a trained therapist, co-counsellors can, after an initial period of training, take it in turns to counsel and be counselled.

Also known as re-evaluation counselling, co-counselling began in the 1960s and emphasizes the need to discharge painful emotions from the past, such as anger, loneliness or resentment, which may be blocking progress in the present. It understands that life cannot proceed properly until we have been able to 'unpack' negative emotions from the past. The person acting as counsellor helps the client to recognize emotions which may have been cut off or hidden or repressed, and to bring them to the surface where they can be harmlessly released. Then, after a certain length of time, client and counsellor change places.

Anybody interested in learning the techniques of co-counselling first has to attend a forty-hour 'fundamentals' course and study a manual. Those taking the fundamentals courses are always people who have been in co-counselling for many years. Participants will learn what it means to be a counsellor: not to comment, give advice, sympathize or share experiences, but just to listen in an empathetic way. What the counsellor should not do, however, is to allow the client to get away with self-deprecatory phrases such as 'I have a short fuse' or 'I flare up easily'. These are all, according to co-counselling, phrases which have been instilled into us at some point, usually by an adult, and have become self-fulfilling prophecies. They are not, though, *us* – or even aspects of us.

Nobody has a 'short fuse' or 'flares up easily' unless they want to, and unless they have come to believe that this is what they are like. Co-counselling teaches that we are all basically loving, giving, positive and nurturing, and that if we don't seem to be so it is because of some hurt that has happened to us in the past. By discharging it, we need no longer live our lives by these outdated and unhelpful scripts.

The whole idea of co-counselling is to demystify the

121

therapeutic process. By acting alternately as counsellor and client, each person learns what is involved and what 'therapy' means – that is, for it to be successful the client has to do all the work.

Once the training is over, people can get together and meet once a week or so for a couple of hours, for as long as both seem to benefit from the arrangement. In co-counselling, no money changes hands – both counsellor and client give their time freely. There is, though, a charge for the fundamentals course, which can also put people in touch with a whole network of co-counsellors all over the world as it is a worldwide movement.

Co-counselling is particularly suitable for people who feel they need to discharge strong but negative emotions from the past. It is for ordinary people who would like a chance to sort out their lives and talk things over with a sympathetic listener. This is not the same as wallowing in misery – the idea is that whatever may be bothering you comes to the surface and is released. It is not intended for the mentally ill, or as an alternative to psychiatric care.

Three basic areas are addressed in co-counselling: relationships, work and lifestyle. And because so many people experience continuing problems in their intimate relationships, this is an extremely important area of co-counselling.

If there appears to be no rapport between you and your co-counsellor, or if the sessions do not seem to be helpful, you can ask to be put in touch with somebody else. There are supervisors who organize the networks and who can put you in touch with somebody more suitable.

Co-counselling is not the same as talking to a friend, because the listener is wholeheartedly concentrating on you, letting you talk, and not interspersing judgements or unhelpful comments. Most people who have been involved in co-counselling admit that it is extremely difficult to listen properly and give somebody your whole attention without losing concentration, without bringing the conversation back to you, and without putting in your own experiences.

For many people, co-counselling is the first time they have ever been properly listened to – and it can be a heady experience. The major factor in this form of counselling is that it enables people to lose their long-held fears and mistrust of others. If somebody has ever treated you badly, or you believe they have treated you badly, then trust may be lost for the future. But if you can believe that people treat you badly because they are in such pain themselves, you can acquire greater understanding and wallow less in the 'victim' role which those who have suffered from obsessive love believe themselves to be playing. Co-counselling very much helps people not to see themselves as victims any more.

It can also help people to open up, to trust others, to talk about themselves, to relate positively to other people. Relationships between co-counsellors are more than just friendship, but are not intimate or 'sexy'. Sometimes co-counsellors will be of the same gender, sometimes opposite.

Non-sexual touch, such as hugging, is also very much encouraged, and co-counsellors may hold hands or touch in other appropriate ways. All this helps to break down the isolation which results when you do not feel you are properly connecting to other people, and have to preserve some kind of false persona about yourself.

One major advantage of co-counselling is that a whole galaxy of potential therapists is on offer. But as with any other relationship, you will click with some people and not so well with others. When this happens, you can ask the area supervisor to put you in touch with somebody else – and the other person will do the same. Sometimes co-counselling relationships go on for years. If distress or a problem surface at a particular time, you can contact your co-counsellor and not have to worry about not being able to afford the therapy, or about bothering a busy therapist with what may seem a trivial matter.

To be a good counsellor, it is essential to be able to both talk and listen well. Not everybody is a naturally good listener, but listening is a skill which can be learnt. And people who may have bottled things up for years start to open out during co-counselling.

Results of therapy

Sometimes the results can be disturbing at first. Don't expect all
to be peace and light and instant enlightenment and forgiveness.
You may be extremely surprised at the strength of your emotions, by your own reactions and by the recognition that the
trauma is still affecting you, maybe years later.

Bear in mind that releasing long-held traumas has much
in common with withdrawing from a powerful mind-altering
drug – there may be initial reluctance to let the old hurt go,
a desire to hang on to it, especially if it seems to have become
part of you over the years, and a reluctance to face up to
reality and to stop blaming somebody else for the hurt and
misery that were caused.

But gradually you will come through and there will be a
feeling of lightness, positiveness and benevolence as never before.
One of the initial effects of releasing traumas, people find, is
that extra energy is accessed. Sometimes this may take the form
of feeling more sexy, as if numbness is being gradually replaced
by feeling. People who have been abused as children often go
completely numb as far as sex is concerned, and also as far as
feelings are concerned. Of course, obsessive love constitutes a
similar kind of abuse, even if it is self-abuse.

The feelings of disturbance, which can be likened to throwing
a stone into a stagnant pond, are in themselves often a good
thing. They mean that emotions, empathy and connectedness
are all coming back; everything is being unfrozen.

There will also usually be a feeling that the defences erected
over the years are no longer necessary. Those who have
alienated others by appearing to be cold and unfeeling, or
by putting on a mask of wit and repartee in order to distance
themselves from other people, will come to feel closer to the
rest of humanity.

The other major positive outcome of therapy is that fears
about other people fade away. Others are not deliberately
out to hurt you, to do you down, nor do they single you
out specially for bad treatment, even though that is how it
often appears when there is obsessive love.

Through successful therapy we can learn not to be hard on ourselves, not to blame either ourselves or others for past misfortunes, and to let the past go so that its shadows no longer adversely affect the present. Some people believe that we start to let go of old hurts and slights and emotional wounds when we need all the energy we can get to face the future.

7 The Past-life Possibility

Is there more to obsessive love?

There is no doubt that the trauma of obsessive love can be released through effective therapy or counselling. But the fact remains that, despite many theories, much soul-searching, nobody has yet been able to get quite to the bottom of the phenomenon.

However much we try to define it and pin it down, it remains elusive, mysterious. One psychotherapist who conducts 'Women Who Love Too Much' workshops and groups, said that, although relationship addiction can now be properly understood in terms of a dysfunctional childhood background, obsessive love seems to elude such an explanation.

Why the one individual?

Although with hindsight we can perhaps point to factors in childhood which increase susceptibility, such as feeling different and special, as noted earlier, the thing that remains mysterious is: why this particular person? After all, most people are fixated only by one individual, not with a whole series of people one after the other.

Relationship addicts always form liaisons with people who, they feel, can be rescued from themselves. Those obsessively in love have no corresponding need to 'rescue' their lovers. We do not make a beeline for addicts, alcoholics, rakes, sexaholics

126

or other 'exciting' people. Although our lovers seem exciting to us, they are not exciting *because* of an addiction or other darkly glamorous personality disorder, such as being a gambler. Of course, they may be these things − but that is not the reason for our overwhelming attraction to them.

Whereas relationship addicts are attracted to the actual dysfunction rather than the person, and love these people especially *because* they are addicts or needy people, we − the obsessed ones − are attracted to the person, to what we see. Those of us who have ever been obsessively in love know that it's always love at first sight, or at first knowledge. Elizabeth Smart, for instance, fell in love with George Barker the person on reading his poems for the first time. She had no idea then what kind of individual he was − but as soon as she met him, the obsession was complete. Her whole life became dedicated to him.

Similarly, Kathleen Raine fell desperately in love with Gavin Maxwell at first sight. With obsessive love, there is no gradual unfolding, no gradual strengthening of feelings. Everything is there at once. And we have to remember that we are falling in love with somebody we don't even know. In many cases, the strength of the obsession will actually stop us from getting to know them properly − they may not live up to the fantasy we have erected, so it may be better to keep a distance.

The strongest feeling to emerge with obsessive love is a certainty that *we already know this person*. We never feel we are meeting a stranger. That is what makes it all so highly odd − we feel we are meeting not an unknown person, but somebody we already know; yet we don't know this person at all in reality.

One explanation could be that those prone to obsessive love have already built in their minds a composite, complete picture of the kind of person they would like to fall in love with, and so the first person who falls vaguely into that blueprint becomes the object of their passion. I wanted to fall in love with a tall, dark, handsome, mysterious, Byronic, rakish, glamorous, confident, sexually experienced, literary, bohemian, adventurous, intelligent, anarchic, travelled, upper-class, educated, available male, someone who smoked and drank and was uninhibited, fun and slightly saturnine at the same time − and John seemed to fit wonderfully into every one of those categories.

Perhaps every young woman wants, or secretly wants, that kind of man — he is, after all, the archetypal romantic hero. But at the time it had never occurred to me that I could inculcate any qualities I wanted for myself, rather than trying to find them in somebody else.

But even this doesn't quite explain it all. It doesn't explain why there should be such overwhelming obsession, such masochistic preoccupation with this person, such a willingness to experience overwhelming misery and agony, such isolation, longing and frustration.

I have been here before

So I am left wondering whether there could be another explanation — if we believe we know this person so well, then perhaps we have already known them in another life. Kathleen Raine strongly believed that her love for Gavin Maxwell arose so instantly because she recognized that they had been very close in another life, maybe as brother and sister. She makes this suggestion quite seriously in her book *The Lion's Mouth*. Gavin Maxwell himself, of course, admitted no such connection. The image of Kathleen Raine that comes over in the film *Ring of Bright Water* (where she was played by Vivien Merchant) is that she is mad, unhinged.

A few years ago, I would not even have considered the past-life possibility seriously, as it would have seemed ridiculously cranky. Anyway, it was something that did not have the merest shred of proof. It was a nice poetic idea, maybe, but one which could not be put to any kind of test.

Now, although there is no concrete proof, a body of evidence is accumulating, difficult to ignore, that we may have more than just the one physical life. There have been numerous examples of people remembering past lives. Although some of these may be fantasies or fakes, are they all? There are also numerous examples of small children, aged two or three, passing cemeteries and saying to their startled parents: 'That's where I was buried.'

Reincarnation is after all an extremely ancient doctrine,

common to all early religions and never finally disproved. It is intimately connected to the idea of karma, the Sanskrit word for action which has come to mean: as you sow, so shall you reap. According to this doctrine, if we meet somebody we seem to know instantly, and with whom there seems a particular rapport, the chances are that we have previously set in motion some kind of karma, which needs to be worked out further in this particular incarnation. Whether the other person responds or not, he or she too has karma connecting to the obsessed one.

All nonsense – or the only explanation which makes sense?

A connection with transsexuality?

In a way, I see obsessive love as having something in common with the strange phenomenon of transsexuality, where people firmly believe, against all the physical evidence, that they are 'really' of the opposite gender. Again, there has never been a satisfactory explanation of transsexuality.

In the past, psychiatrists have tried to interpret transsexuality as the result of an absent father and over-protective mother, or of a situation where the parents have desperately wanted a child of the other sex. But as investigations proceeded it was found that few transsexuals fitted into this category – they come from absolutely all backgrounds, educational levels, cultures and societies. The latest theory is that something goes wrong inside the brain during the crucial time for foetal development, in that the body becomes that of a normal female or male, but the brain has undergone different 'wiring', so that the body and brain are not in harmony.

There may well be something in this theory – but as yet it remains theory. However investigations by Professor Ian Stevenson, of the University of Virginia, have revealed that many children who cannot accept their gender were actually of the opposite in a previous life – and those lives came to an untimely end in some way. Transsexuality reveals itself very early in life, before there is any orientation towards homosexuality or heterosexuality.

It may well be that obsessive love has some kind of similar

129

origin – that two people who had a connection in a previous life have to come together in some way to finish business or sever the connection of this present life.

If there is anything in this explanation it does not, of course, rule out any of the other factors which appear to apply, such as feelings of alienation, isolation and vulnerability, the 'urge to merge', the childhood experiences leading to feeling different and unconnected with family, our cultural expectations regarding falling in love, the propensity some women have for falling in love with their teachers or therapists, or that certain men have to fall for very young, 'pure' girls.

But the thing which remains strange is the fixation on a particular person. For instance, some biographers of Charlotte Brontë have attempted to explain her adoration of Heger by saying that, given her childhood experiences of a remote father, dead mother and distant aunt, and isolated, hothouse childhood and urgent need to make something of her life, it was hardly surprising that she would fall desperately in love with the first 'real' man she met. Yet Emily, who wrote passionately about obsessive love in *Wuthering Heights*, and who had identical childhood experiences to Charlotte, did not even begin to fall in love with Heger. Nor did Charlotte ever fall in love with anybody else – not even men who were more suitable, or more available. So what was it?

I've never been obsessively in love with anybody except John, even though I have met plenty of other people who would have been more responsive, more helpful to me in my career, more likely to return the affection. Why him, as I asked myself in my teenage diaries?

If it were merely childhood influences at work, surely we would be tempted to repeat the pattern, as relationship addicts do? Surely we would find one person after another to be obsessed by – and who did not return the affection? For most of us, though, once is enough.

The common pattern is that we have an obsession with somebody and the feelings are not returned; then in time it all seems to go away and we settle down with somebody else, telling ourselves that now we are happy and that the other person was no good for us anyway. Yet they are always there at the back of our minds, and tending to come forward, rather than retreating into the dim and distant past, as the years go by. They keep impinging, for some reason – they won't ever quite go away. Whether or not there is, or has been, any actual relationship, is beside the point.

Past-life therapy

How likely is it that those we love obsessively are people we have known in some previous incarnation? Certainly, anybody who believes in reincarnation and karma would say that it is the only possible explanation. But it is not an idea taken seriously by most psychiatrists or psychoanalysts, who are anxious to explain everything in terms of childhood experiences of one sort or another. However, the blinding flash of recognition, the cataclysmic instant falling in love – *with this particular person* – which characterizes the phenomenon has so far defied any plausible explanation. And certainly, although poets and novelists have wonderfully and accurately described the agonies of obsessive love, they have never been able to account for it.

My own therapy at Morning Light included a past-life session, to see whether this might shed any light on my strange obsession with John. Veronica Stephenson has come to believe in reincarnation during the fifteen years she has been working as a regression therapist. She said: 'It happened by accident, really. We are basically a Christian foundation, and did not initially see ourselves meddling with things like past lives. But as we took people back in time, they began to tell us things which could not have happened in their present lives.

'It began to happen so often that in the end we were forced to accept it. Now, past-life therapy is a standard form of treatment for those who want it.'

Veronica thought it was possible that when I first met John in the snack-bar queue this activated a memory which belonged to something much farther back than the impact of his attractiveness, self-confidence, stylish appearance, ineffable glamour – and my wish to fall overwhelmingly in love and be swept off my feet. This apparent past life was recalled under exactly the same conditions as the ordinary regression therapy.

I was lying down, covered with a blanket, while Veronica sat beside me and asked questions. The whole session was tape recorded.

I was not hypnotized, but as the session proceeded I went into a slightly altered state of consciousness, where I knew exactly what I was saying but could not alter or modify it in any way.

To those who believe that past lives are all nonsense, and that we make up what we want people to hear or are using our imaginations, I would say that it seemed impossible to make anything up. What came out came out, and I seemed powerless to change it in any way.

When Veronica asked my name, I said it seemed to be the same as in this life: Elizabeth. I came from quite a wealthy Victorian family and had nothing much to do except visit friends' houses and wait for a suitable man who would ask for my hand in marriage. In the event I resisted marriage until my late twenties, when a much older man pursued me with great vigour and dedication.

I was not in love with him, but eventually succumbed and married him, The marriage was not happy, and did not work out. There were no children. My elderly husband seemed to change character when we married and became dour, humourless and harsh.

I longed for some genuine experience of love, and eventually a young man appeared on the scene. The details were hazy, but it appears that we enjoyed a blissful relationship which included sex. The affair was highly dangerous because in those days there was simply no way of divorcing or getting rid of my husband, so it all had to be conducted in deadly secret.

My lover was quite a lot younger than me, and only twenty-three when I met him. I described him as being full of enthusiasm and humour — and remarked that, although I had seemed such a serious person, there was a fun side to my character which had never come out with my elderly husband. I could remember thinking as I described this life that it sounded very much like the plot of George Eliot's *Middlemarch*, one of my favourite novels, and I wondered whether I was simply adapting this plot rather than genuinely describing a life of my own.

Of course there can be no real way of telling, but the outcome of my relationship with my young lover was a positive one. Although my elderly dried-up husband did not conveniently die, as did Mr Casaubon in *Middlemarch*, enabling Dorothea to marry her young lover Will Ladislaw, he became less and less important as the years went by.

Eventually my young lover went away, married and had a family of his own, as there could be no future in my relationship with him. I mentioned during the therapy that I felt liberated with this young man and could be myself with him in a way that was impossible with my husband. He was, I said, like a breath of fresh air and with him I did not feel I was walled up in prison, as I did when with my husband.

The wonderful thing, I said, was that we were able to share on all levels and that we seemed meant for each other. The physical relationship was wonderful, but most of all we could enjoy laughter together.

After my lover had gone the liberation I had experienced in his company seemed to open doors, and eventually I became quite a pillar of the community. I wrote books. I became in some way a person of influence, although in exactly what way remains unclear.

The session finished with me dying as a very old lady and describing my death, which was not at all frightening but opened from a long dark tunnel into light.

The interpretation

To me, this rather tedious past life seemed to have no relevance at all to my present existence − or my obsessive relationship. Veronica suggested the following connection: there was not an immediately obvious tie-up, she said, but it seemed as if a sense of liberation was the key factor.

At first, she said, she had thought that the elderly husband might be an aspect of John, but then thought this didn't seem to fit at all. It was far more likely that he was the young man with whom I'd enjoyed such a blissful relationship, yet it had to be cut short because of the *mores* of the time. It was a dangerous liaison which could not continue. This young man, said Veronica, enabled me to blossom into a laughing, alive person, when I had felt dead, constrained with my husband. He opened a door so that things were never the same again.

'The blinding flash when you saw John,' she said, 'could have been the blinding flash of recognition, a feeling that he was going to open doors for you and that the relationship would be, in some way, extraordinary.'

I remained unconvinced. How could John have liberated me, when my relationship with him was full of such agony and despair, so different from the one described in this previous life?

Veronica said: 'It seems to me that in your present life John acted as a catalyst which enabled you to make the final break with your past, your childhood.

'During your childhood you hadn't been able to be yourself, had always felt set apart from your family, and you couldn't be yourself with him either. After the affair with him finished, there was, broadly speaking, a pattern of achievement and purpose, a goal which was never lost, even though of course there were setbacks and disappointments.'

A slight bell rang here. It was true that I had never been able to be myself in my childhood home and felt like a changeling in the 'respectable' but uncultured and non-nurturing working-class background of my early years. Because of this I had developed, or had tried to develop, a sophisticated, glamorous persona, a cold, hard exterior which would leave me invulnerable. I also tried to pretend, at university, that I was much better read, better travelled, more knowledgeable than I really was. This fragile sense of identity was all to be shattered not long after meeting John.

And I could not in any way be myself with him. In fact, it seemed as if I had never been myself – whatever 'myself' was. But not long after the affair ended I met Neville, and with him was able truly to relax. With him I did not feel I had to play any kind of part or pretend to be what I wasn't. I got on with him and established a rapport right from the start.

It was unfortunate, perhaps, that I fell so deeply in love with John when I had no rapport at all with him (although a degree was established at our subsequent meeting) and that, although I got on so well with Neville from the start, there was no blinding flash, no desperate love there.

'Your relationship with John,' Veronica continued, 'catapulted you into a cocoon of distress, illness and misery, and you emerged stronger for it. If John had been caring and loving, as you wanted, you might never have gained the strength to become independent and achieving.

'You might have felt that he was unkind and unjust, but because of the suffering you were enabled to shed the skin of your previous life and emerge from the chrysalis into the butterfly. The relationship, and its effect on you, enabled you to discover colours in yourself which might never otherwise have emerged.

'Because he had a strong personality and was striking, you might have lived in his shadow if a proper relationship had been established. You might never have become equal, never shone in your own right. You might have continued to be the "little woman" and not very confident of yourself.

'You lost your identity for a time with John, and the shock of recognizing him had the effect of fragmenting your awareness. But you had a strong memory of something extremely positive in the past, and you were responding to that.'

But — why should John not have responded when, apparently, the relationship had been reciprocated in the previous existence?

Veronica said: 'As I see it, the soul energy was now clothed with a different identity, and a different personality. Your soul energy recognised his energy, and the memory acted as a springboard.

'My feeling is that each incarnation brings its opportunities for growth on all levels. If every blissful relationship picked up where it left off in the previous incarnation, I really do think it would be inhibiting.

'I think we have to be able to step back from our experiences in order to learn from them. But, far from being a negative experience, you can now see it as extremely positive. Until recently, you were unable to get the effects of the memory of him out of your system, so that every now and again a memory would keep returning. Now, you are no longer a victim of that memory. You can shed it once and for all.

'You are no longer a victim of somebody else's powerful personality, and although John took your power away from you for a time, you've reclaimed it and the knot is completely untied.

I asked Veronica what she meant by John taking my power away from me.

'Whenever you are overwhelmed by an obsession,' she said, 'you no longer seem to have any power over your actions or thoughts. It seems as if the other person has you in thrall, and that you have lost the ability to think and act rationally. Getting over the obsession is, really, a matter of reclaiming your power over yourself.'

She continued: 'If the blissful experience of the previous life had been repeated, it might not have been so positive in this life. You would have been remembering rather than reliving, so it wouldn't have been so good.'

Veronica felt that, in responding so overwhelmingly to John's presence and aura, I was possessed by strong energies from a previous existence. Certainly I have never had a feeling like that at any other time in my life. I was completely taken over by it, powerless to do anything about it or keep it under control.

Memories, said Veronica, are energies, and as such they can be extremely powerful. 'Now you are not a prisoner of the past any more, and you can let it all go. It has no power over you any more.'

Analysis

Accurate analysis — or so much mumbo-jumbo? It all depends on your particular viewpoint. Those who have fervently set their minds against the idea of reincarnation, and feel there is no logical explanation for such a belief, will think it is full of holes.

How could anybody be sure that the young man was John? How could anybody be sure that I was describing my own past life, rather than just a standard Victorian existence? Of course, there can be no such certainties. I might have been plundering the depths of my imagination or memory — there can be no proof that I was actually calling up a past life.

On the other hand, the *explanation* makes sense. Veronica Stephenson asks: 'How can you seem to fall in love with somebody you don't know and have never met before – unless you already *have* met that person?' And it was certainly true that after the experience I made up my mind that never would I fall so low again, never would I get so out of control again. There *was* liberation, a new sense of confidence, a feeling of emerging into some kind of light after the darkness and desperation of my obsession.

But of course, Veronica could have been speaking with hindsight – after all, by the time we came to the past-life session we had already had several sessions of therapy together, plus an initial talk, so she knew me pretty well by now. She could have been simply sensibly tying up loose ends, putting a positive explanation on what happened.

And why, if there was some close connection in a previous life, does only one person ever seem to feel it?

Veronica's explanation here is that with each new incarnation the soul is clothed in different energies. We each have our own individual lessons to learn, each individual's karma is different, and so there would not be repetition in a new incarnation. It may have been that, although I had something to learn from the experience in this life with John, he did not have a corresponding lesson to learn from me.

It may also be that there is non-reciprocity because of fear. When he met me again, John admitted that the original encounter had been painful and traumatic for him. It was significant too, that when I contacted him initially he could not remember me at all, yet his ex-wife, a woman I had never spoken to in my life and never met, had a very clear recollection of me and knew exactly who I was.

John also had an extremely clear picture of my ex-husband – again, somebody he had never spoken to or had any communication with. So why should these memories surface readily, when he had apparently no memory of the person who haunted and stalked him for months on end, and whom he deflowered? The answer here is that maybe he too was blocking out something hurtful or painful.

Who can tell what the explanation is? But as the outcome for me was not insignificant, it seems that we can't absolutely dismiss the possibility of the past-life impingement. If we are, as many religions believe, here to learn valuable lessons, and if painful experiences give us the chance to learn those lessons, then the past-life idea seems to make some kind of sense.

It seems unlikely that something as all-consuming as obsessive love should be a matter of mere chance. According to the doctrine of karma, the reason we meet people again – although they may be in a different relationship to us this time, or of a different sex – is because there is unfinished business, because there are still lessons to learn from the relationship, or because there is karma to be completed. But we will never merely repeat what happened in a previous incarnation. This time round, things will be different – which is why the relationship may so often be one-sided.

Each participant in the relationship will have a completely different karma. Also, if there has been some unresolved difficulty in one life there may be new difficulties in the present one – but we will always be given the opportunity to resolve those difficulties.

According to ancient doctrine, karma can be of three kinds – good, bad and neutral. Whenever we mistreat somebody in a previous life we have caused bad karma which will rebound on us inexorably at some time. According to this belief, if John treated me badly in this life (or I believed he treated me badly, which amounts to much the same thing), that means I must have enacted some karma with him which must be paid off.

Accordingly, by his treatment of me John will have set some karma into being which he will then have to repay in some way. It may have been that John and I had some joint karma (according to the ancient doctrine) and that, for some reason we needed each other at the time in order to learn important lessons.

The fact that he did not respond to me in the way I wanted does not mean that no karma was set into being. There was obviously something about him which made me respond to him in an obsessive and besotted way, and the nature of his response would affect his own karma for the future.

If there has been good karma, one can assume that the business is now finished and that there will be no more interaction between the protagonists. In neutral karma the outcome is neither good nor bad, such as when we meet casual acquaintances on holiday whose company we enjoy for a while but then never see them again.

Those who have an understanding of karma would appreciate that the circumstances which set into being my eventual meeting with John were also no chance occurrences, but a swift completion of whatever business or emotions existed between us. Why should he, for example, have been in the UK, and therefore easy to contact, just when I needed to contact him – when in fact he lives in the Far East? Was it also pure luck that by the time we met again both of us were divorced, and so had the freedom to meet and talk? It wouldn't have been so easy with possessive spouses in the background.

I can't know the answers to all these questions – because it must, at the moment, rest on guesswork. All I can know for certain is how different I feel, having resolved my own problem of obsessive love – and having it all, in the end, made easy for me.

The 'past-life' explanation is that John appeared on the scene at a time when I needed to learn some important, perhaps searing, lessons about myself. Because, through intense suffering and agony, I managed to learn the lessons, they were not repeated – and I did not ever fall hopelessly in love again.

The effect was to enable me to become stronger, so that I could survive. And, although the survival mechanism of not allowing my feelings to be deeply engaged had been helpful over the years, I had now got to the point where this mechanism was getting in the way, stopping me from making further progress. So it had to be sorted out. The spectre of the relationship came up again, and refused to go away until I had dealt with it.

'Sometimes,' said Veronica Stephenson, 'we have to become less than ourselves to become more of ourselves. Your illusions about yourself, your sense of identity, were all shattered soon after meeting John. But you put yourself back together in a far more functional way.'

It seems to me that the jury is still out with the past-life explanation – but it does have a logic and attraction about it which other theories simply don't possess. That doesn't necessarily make it true, of course, but the past-life possibility does not negate any of the other explanations and theories which may account for obsessive love – in fact, to me it adds to them, and seems to complete the whole story.

Conclusion

Everybody's experience of obsessive love is slightly different. The overwhelming characteristic is one of need – you seem to need this person so desperately. And although obsessive love is not real love, it has something in common with love, because you long to be with this person, you long to have a wonderful relationship, you feel so strongly that this is the only individual who really matters.

There is a saying that it's better to have loved and lost than never to have loved at all. And I think if you were to ask anybody who has ever been desperately in love if they would rather it had never happened, they would say no. It is a vivid and dramatic experience, even if uncomfortable for most of the time. And of course, for most of us who have ever been in love in this way, there are also moments of wonder as well.

The experience is not something most of us would wish to repeat – indeed, could the human frame stand it? And even though it may be 99 per cent agony, it contains glimpses of bliss which never quite seem to come again in life.

It's certainly not all negative. We know what it's like to come alive in the loved one's presence, to be thrilled by the mere sight or thought of this person, to have despair turned to delight when there is even a hint of reciprocity. Life is certainly not mundane for those desperately in love – it is momentarily lifted to some higher, or at least other, plane of existence.

Yes, obsessive love is stressful, traumatic, a shock to the system. But at the time it is also extremely exciting. The danger comes, though, not so much from the trauma itself, as from our reaction to it, and when we never seem to get over it. And the greatest danger is when our uncontrollable love turns to hate — because the feelings are not returned — and when lasting feelings of hostility and resentment, coupled with guilt and shame, are allowed to stay in the system for years on end. But, with understanding of what is involved in obsessive love, these feelings can be released and removed so that they no longer have the power to affect the present and future.

We cannot always choose not to fall hopelessly in love. But we can choose not to let the experience affect our capacity for genuine love. We can cut the ties that once bound us so tightly, free ourselves from the lingering traces of negative attachment, and face the future with confidence, self-esteem and a true sense of our own autonomous identity.

Resources

Alexander technique

The Society of Teachers of the Alexander Technique
10 London House
266 Fulham Road
London SW10 9EL
(Tel: 071-351 0828)

Autogenic training

Dr Malcolm Carruthers
British Association for Autogenic Training
The Positive Health Centre
101 Harley Street
London W1
(Tel: 071-935 1811)

Dr Kai Kermani
Loughton Centre for Autogenic Training
10 Connaught Hill
Loughton
Essex
IG10 4DU
(Tel: 0943 463217)

Counselling and psychotherapy

The British Association for Counselling
37a Sheep Street
Rugby
Warwicks
CV21 3BX

Human Potential Research Project (*Co-counselling*)
Dept of Educational Studies
University of Surrey
Guildford
Surrey
GU2 5XH
(Tel: 048 509 191)

Westminster Pastoral Foundation (*information on counselling*)
23 Kensington Square
London W8

The College of Psychic Studies
16 Queensbury Place
London SW7
(Tel: 071-589 3292)

British Psychodrama Association (*working through unresolved blocks and traumas through acting out the scene*)
113 Herschel Crescent
Littlemore
Oxford
OX4 3TX

The Institute of Dramatherapy
37 Chalk Farm Road
London NW1 8AJ
(Tel: 071-267 9649)

The British Association of Psychotherapists
121 Hendon Lane
London N3 3PR
(Tel: 081-346 1747)

Morning Light Holiday Retreat and Healing Centre
Dalcroy Farm
Tummel Bridge
By Pitlochry
Perth
PH16 5NT
(Tel: 08824 230)

Dr Francesca Rossetti
Flat 5
41 Lansdowne Road
London W11
(Tel: 071-792 2957)

Soul-Directed Astrology
5 Cedar Road
Sutton
Surrey
SM2 5DA
(Tel: 081-643 4898)

Soul-Directed Therapy
Dr Lisa Sand and Mrs Inga Hooper
17b Cedar Road
Sutton
Surrey
(Tel: 081-643 4255)

Spiritual healing

National Federation of Spiritual Healers
Old Manor Farm Studio
Church Street
Sunbury-on-Thames
Middlesex
TW16 6RG
(Tel: 09327 83164/5)

Meditation

Meditation courses are held by:
The Sivananda Yoga Vedanta Centre
(*address in yoga section*)

The Brahma Kumaris World Spiritual University
(*address in yoga section*)

Circle dancing

Judy King
75 Newtown Road
Eastleigh
Hants
SO5 4BX
(Tel: 0703 641632)

Massage

Clare Maxwell-Hudson
87 Dartmouth Road
London NW2 4ER
(Tel: 081-450 6494)

Past-life therapy

The Hypnothink Foundation
PO Box 154
Cheltenham
Glos
GL53 9EG

Yoga

British Wheel of Yoga
1 Hamilton Place
Boston Road
Sleaford
Lincs
NG34 7ES
(Tel: 0529 306851)

The Brahma Kumaris World Spiritual University
98 Tennyson Road
London NW6 7SB
(Tel: 081-450 5563)

The Sivananda Yoga Vedanta Centre
51 Felsham Road
London SW15 1AZ
(Tel: 081-780 0160)

The Yoga for Health Foundation
Ickwell Bury
Ickwell Green
Biggleswade
Beds SG18 9EF
(Tel: 0767 27271)

Obsessive Love

The Iyengar Institute
223a Randolph Avenue
London W9
(Tel: 071-624 3080)

Further Reading

Brennan, J. H. *Understanding Reincarnation* (Aquarian, 1990)

Hodgkinson, Liz *Spiritual Healing* (Piatkus, 1990)

Hodgkinson, Liz *Reincarnation* (Piatkus, 1989)

Kasl, Charlotte Davis *Women, Sex and Addiction* (Mandarin, 1990)

Kermani, Dr Kai *Autogenic Training* (Souvenir Press, 1990)

Lidell, Lucy *The Book of Yoga* (Ebury Press, 1983)

Markham, Ursula, *Hypnosis Regression Therapy and How It Can Help You* (Piatkus, 1991)

Maxwell, Gavin *Raven Seek Thy Brother* (Longmans, 1968)

Maxwell, Gavin *Ring of Bright Water* (Longmans, 1960)

Miller, Alice *The Untouched Key: Tracing Childhood Trauma in Creativity and Destructiveness* (Virago, 1990)

Peck, M. Scott *The Road Less Travelled* (Rider, 1983)

Person, Ethel Spector *Love and Fateful Encounters: The Power of Romantic Passion* (Bloomsbury, 1989)

Raine, Kathleen *The Lion's Mouth* (Hamish Hamilton, 1977)

Smart, Elizabeth *By Grand Central Station I Sat Down and Wept* (Paladin, 1991)

Smart, Elizabeth *Necessary Secrets* (Grafton, 1991)

Woolger, Dr Roger *Other Lives, Other Selves: A Jungian Psychotherapist Discovers Past Lives* (Crucible, 1990)

Ziegler, Philip *King Edward VIII: The Official Biography* (Collins, 1990)

Index

Piatkus Books

If you are interested in recovery, health and personal growth, you may like to read other titles published by Piatkus.

Adult Children of Divorce: How to achieve happier relationships Dr Edward W. Beal and Gloria Hochman

The Alexander Technique: How it can help you Liz Hodgkinson

The Chosen Child Syndrome: What to do when a parent's love rules your life Dr Patricia Love and Jo Robinson

Codependents' Guide to the Twelve Steps: How to understand and follow a recovery programme Melody Beattie

Codependency: How to break free and live your own life David Stafford and Liz Hodgkinson

The Encyclopaedia of Alternative Health Care: The complete guide to choices in healing Kristin Olsen

Homecoming: Reclaiming and championing your inner child John Bradshaw

Hypnosis Regression Therapy and How it Can Help You Ursula Markham

Increase Your Energy: Regain your zest for life the natural way Louis Proto

Opening Our Hearts to Men: Taking charge of our lives and creating a love that works Susan Jeffers

The Power of Gems and Crystals: How they can transform your life Soozi Holbeche

Self-Healing: How to use your mind to heal your body Louis Proto

The Shiatsu Workbook: A beginners' guide Nigel Dawes

Spiritual Healing: Everything you want to know Liz Hodgkinson

Stress Control Through Self Hypnosis Dr Arthur Jackson

Super Massage: Simple techniques for instant relaxation Gordon Inkeles

For a free brochure with further information on our range of titles, please write to:

Piatkus Books
Freepost 7 (WD 4505)
London W1E 4EZ

PIATKUS